Bright Business Transformation

For Contractors

EMERSON PATTON

CONKERPRESS

ISBN: 9798359099035

FOREWORD

Around four years ago I went looking for a coach and used Google and LinkedIn to search for one. That was how I came across Emerson and Bright. Our first contact was by phone and I liked what I heard during the call so we arranged to meet for a pub lunch. Over beer and a burger, Emerson showed me his model and when he was about halfway through I stopped him. I didn't need to hear anymore as it was exactly what I'd been looking for, almost as if it had been designed for me personally.

At work, we got stuck in. It was intense seeing results straight away. This spurred us on and there followed an eighteen-month rollercoaster! What we went through in those eighteen months was a complete business transformation in everything we were doing. We followed the system and implemented it all to make all of it work better. Now we are positioned to grow sustainably, and every member of our team is engaged.

When I heard this book was happening, I knew it was a no brainer. By transferring the expertise and methods in this way, it's like giving you the keys to the kingdom. The best way to explain it is it's like trying to do a jigsaw without having seen the image on the box. That is what Emerson does – he hands you the lid, so that you can clearly see what to do. I'd say to any contractor who is looking for a coach, read this book first. I guarantee that by following the 7 Sector Model you will change your business for the better.

Before I did this, I was working sixty plus hours a week and was run ragged, chasing my tail, struggling with suppliers and falling out with my team. Now I work ten to fifteen hours a week, draw a salary and have the time to get involved with other things. The best one of all is walking my daughter to school. You just can't put a price on that.

Paul Gedney – Owner & Managing Director at R J Wilson

BRIGHT BUSINESS TRANSFORMATION

'For a man to conquer himself is the first and noblest of all victories.' - Plato

HOW TO USE THIS BOOK FOR THE BEST RESULTS

If you go to our resources page at the back of the book (chapter 9), you will see a set of QR codes that will take you to our website. There you will find useful tools to help you grow your business. Just hover your smart phone camera app over the QR image to access it. You can also type the web address below into your browser.

https://www.brightbusinessadvice.com/book-resources/

I recommend that you download 'the 7 Sector Orbit Model' to help you better understand the contents of this book and it will help to focus your own business growth journey. To bring a lot of this to life, you can watch the short videos on each of the 7 sectors and I will talk you through them there.

You will also see that I recommend books for you to read, and I do this to help you understand each sector in more detail. These books are where a lot of my inspiration comes from.

Throughout this book and at the back there are also some awesome quotes from inspirational people to really get you thinking.

The book resources page on our website will be continually evolving and we will keep updating it with other useful tools and documents to help you build your business. This will also help us achieve our goal to impact the lives of over 1,000,000 business owners worldwide for the better.

Last but not least, we will list our key partners who are mentioned in this book and if you want to find out more about them or get some free demos, downloads and trials of their services, keep your eye out for them.

I've also left some blank pages at the back of the book so that you can write down the most useful ideas and concepts you come across. There will be many things in here you can work on in your business and so you can make an action list for those 'must do' items.

CONTENTS

Introduction   Pg 2

1   Bright Beginnings   Pg 6

2   Leadership   Pg 29

3   Planning & Management   Pg 64

4   Finance   Pg 85

5   Operations   Pg 110

6   Human Resources   Pg 124

7   Marketing   Pg 154

8   Sales   Pg 175

9   Tools & Resources   Pg 191

10 Results   Pg 196

INTRODUCTION

'If you do what you've always done, you'll get what you've always gotten'

That quote has been credited to the likes of Albert Einstein, Henry Ford, and Tony Robbins. The truth is, there is no verified source of who said it first. Does that really matter? No, I don't think so. What matters is the truth in the words…

This book is about changing the way you think and the way you do things, so that you can get where you want to go in your business. Right now, you drive your business, but who drives you?

One of the most common problems for small to medium sized business owners is that they are so dedicated to their businesses, they spend all their hours working *IN* it, with no time to work *ON* it. Just like they've always done, they roll up their sleeves to get on with the daily deliverables but what they don't realise is, by doing so they may be limiting their growth as a business.

The Bright 7 Sector Model is a system that addresses this problem and helps to transform every business we work with. It is a system I implemented fifteen years ago and since then, I've been streamlining and improving it to keep it current and always moving forward. This model works at optimum level for all my clients and I'm very proud of it.

For any business to thrive, even at a basic level, these seven sectors need to work in conjunction with each other. This builds the foundations for a great business and once the sectors are in place at the first level, you can build with sophistication up through the other five levels, until everything is aligned.

To help explain this model simply, without jargon or complicated technical terms, I have designed it around the human body; an amazing system. It is the perfect working system with all parts working and supporting each other to achieve great things. With this system at our disposal, we humans have been able to achieve great feats of ingenuity and engineering throughout the years. Just think, we have gone from using stone and flint for tools to building airplanes and putting man on the moon. That is why the Bright 7 Sector Model is designed to reflect the incredible machine we live in.

But before we dive in, let me start by giving you an overview.

Don't get stuck on the tools in your business as you will never make real money with a tool in your hand. Real money comes when you're in the office working *on* the business not *in* it. As we say at Bright, *you need to MANAGE the plan, take CONTROL of the systems, team, and finances to GROW the customer base and achieve success.*

1 BRIGHT BEGINNINGS
The distance between your dreams and reality is called ACTION

Again, it's not clear who first said the line above, so I can't quote them, but it's very true and I think you must know that or you wouldn't have picked up this book.

Most of the clients who come to Bright have a business already but the one thing they have in common is that they know they're stuck and are not moving forward. That is because they are stuck working *in* their business, not *on* it. You will hear me say that a lot.

They are working long hours and don't have time to spend on the things they love, like family and friends but they don't want to hand any of the responsibility over to someone else, because they feel no one can do the job as well as they can. The other problem is that often their team, whether it's big or small, are not supportive enough nor do they love their job enough to want to step up.

As a business owner it is your company, your baby and your responsibility and going it alone, trying to do everything yourself is the quickest way to the cemetery. OK. that's a bit dramatic I know but we all know that stress is a killer.

My point is this - getting someone in to guide you works. Someone who has done it for themselves and helped other businesses like yours to do it too, will change your business and your life. Doing that is where you can shorten that distance between your dreams and your reality.

In this book, I am going to show you just how it works. Of course, I can't give you the accountability here in the pages, but you will be able to move forward based on the content and if you do that, you'll be one step closer to your dreams.

Now, before we dive in, I'd like to share a little about my journey with you and explain how I got here today.

Do you remember the 90s? The days of the Sony Discman, the rave culture, the dissolution of the Soviet Union and the dot com bubble? Well, back then, I was a young apprentice, just nineteen years old and living at home with my mum and my stepdad.

I was on the last year of my apprenticeship in electrical and electronic engineering and studying for my NVQ level 4 and HNC. I was also living the life with not a care in the world… well, almost.

Living at home I'd witnessed a few heated rows between my mum and my stepdad, and I didn't really think too much about that. Most people argue, don't they? But one night, I was woken up by shouting and screaming from down the hall and I got out of bed to see what was going on. As I opened my bedroom door and stepped out into the hallway, Mum came flying past me, then used me to shield her. My stepdad was this big guy who looked like Clint Eastwood, with the Dirty Harry attitude too and he was standing in the doorway of their bedroom glaring at us down the hall. His massive frame filled every inch of that door frame and, as it was the middle of the night, it kind of felt like we were in some movie just waiting for it all to kick off.

Here was this guy I'd looked up to, a role model. Someone who had worked very hard to go from apprentice to Electrical Engineer, who'd even being able to afford a Porsche at an early age. He'd always impressed me and up until that night, I had wanted to be like him.

That night though, he was raging. He was shouting at me to get out of the way so that he could get his hands on my mum. I couldn't understand that. My mum is this beautiful little blonde woman – how could anyone want to hurt her? Especially someone who was supposed to love her.

I wouldn't move out of the way and that just made him angrier. He screamed at me repeatedly. *"Who do you think you are? You're not going to amount to anything. You'll do nothing with your life."*

I still hear those words to this day.

That voice is in my head whenever I try to do something to move me forward. It's a voice that tries to trip me up. Tries to stop me getting ahead. It is a trigger but it is also a driver and I used it spur me on because I would not let him win.

I know I'm not the only boy who had that kind of experience. I'm guessing you might have a voice in your head too. It might be one that interrupts you and tells you that you're going to fail, but it has no power over you unless you let it and here, in this book, it's not relevant at all. What I'm sharing with you is tried, tested and proven, so you can't fail … all you must do is to put the work in.

After that night with him and his rage, we packed up and moved. My carefree days were done and I had to step up and become the man of the house. So, I knuckled down, got my qualifications and became an engineer, then I ended up in tech support. Turns out, I was good at helping people sell stuff and so I took what I'd learned and got into the corporate world as a company called Kingston Communications. That was a pivotal moment in my career and there I met Jon Bailey, the boss who became my mentor.

Jon was always reading business books and listening to personal development tapes (yes it was the 90s) and it was something he passed on to me. Over the seven years I worked there, I learned so much from him and my career went from Junior Sales Executive to Senior Account Manager as I became *number one* across the whole country. That felt great but it wasn't the most significant part of the journey. That was still to come.

One day at an appraisal, Jon said to me: "Emerson, you're 186% ahead of target and you're smashing it but what do you want to do next?"

I had to think about that. I just wasn't sure. I'd loved the books and the learnings and running the sales team gave me a buzz, but I did feel there was more for me out there. As I was thinking about this, he asked me the question that changed everything for me:

"Emerson, you need to take the risk of being brilliant."

Wow, I thought. *Take the risk of being brilliant?* I could do that, couldn't I?

Well, I was certainly going to try and I wasn't going to hang around. I went out and looked for that risk, which is when I found 'ActionCoach,' a global firm that had a presence in over fifty countries at that time.

A thousand coaches, working with seventeen thousand businesses on a weekly basis – These were some BIG figures.

To cut a long story short, I got in and became part of that machine. I was proud to be one of the youngest coaches ever to join them and that is how I started my third apprenticeship.

It was all new to me and I didn't really know what I was doing so I thought, why not call some of the most successful coaches around and ask them what they were doing? Yes, it was a bold move on my part I guess, but I was fully up for taking the risk of being brilliant and maybe that was the right attitude, because those people said 'yes'. They talked to me, answered my questions and gave me their advice. I was under their wings and sucking up all the knowledge and information they gave like a sponge - I thrived on it.

The next significant meeting was with George Hannides, a man who became my father figure and my mentor – he was the former Financial Director of Pirelli, where he'd held that position for twenty odd years and I was lucky enough to get him as a work partner. We made a great team, him specialising in finance and me in sales & marketing. Incidentally, it was around this time that I first worked with Doug Wady, who you'll hear about later in this book.

In the first five years at ActionCoach, things were working well, and I did ok. In the second five years however, I started making waves and I won *best client results* three times - 2011, 2012 and 2014 (I must have had sick bug in 2013!). After achieving that level of success, it gave me more confidence and I felt ready to go from apprentice to master, so in 2015, I started my own company and Bright was born.

In our first two years we won several awards and championed our clients to enter awards which they started winning too. It was a great success story but then disaster struck in April 2020 when I lost seventy five percent of my client base overnight due to the pandemic. I know it happened to a lot of people and it may also have happened to you too?

Back then, I didn't know what to do for the best, so I called one of my mentors, Pam Featherstone of the Business Coach Academy. She told me to pivot and take my business online. Up until then, I'd been running big, in-person events with people like the ECA (Electrical Contractors Association), Professional Electrician Magazine and global giant Schneider Electric. I'm a people person and I loved what I did, it all made sense to me, but to do what Pam had told me meant I was supposed to run webinars and become digital. That was some challenge as I'd never run a webinar in my life. I could hear my stepdad in my head and once again, so I used that voice to drive me forward and I joined a webinar mastermind group and invested in my online education. This was with an award-winning entrepreneur and authority in the industry named Paul O'Mahoney.

Since that day, Bright has doubled the size of its business and taken on ten coaches to help keep up with demand.

Don't ever be afraid of investing to move your business forward. Just make sure you invest in the right people and programmes. I wholeheartedly believe that it is what it takes to grow your success and it has worked every time for me.

Now the sky is the limit and I'm on a mission to help other businesses do the same. We're working toward the BIG vision and want to impact the lives of one hundred thousand business owners for the better. We'll do this by coaching ten thousand business owners to create a thousand millionaires through one hundred Bright coaches, over the next ten years. Ambitious but totally doable.

To do that, we need to get moving, just like you do ... so, let's do this!

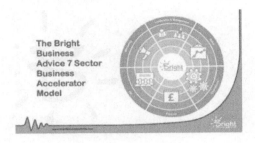

The Bright 7 Sector Business Accelerator Model

When using this model to structure a business, I like to use the human body analogy because the body is one of the best, most sophisticated and powerful interconnected system that nature has ever designed. We humans dominate this planet.

The model has been developed from my experience over the last fifteen years and I use it to transform businesses into highly profitable, efficient and self-sustaining operations.

Let's start at the very top.

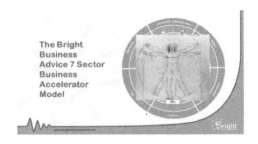

THE HEAD

1 – Leadership

With this analogy, leadership is the head. The right side of the brain focuses on emotion, creativity and connection, and here you develop your knowledge; use eyes to see your vision and your mouth to communicate that vision and strategy to your team. Then you use your ears to listen and learn to engage better with your people. By doing this, it enables you to create a winning mindset, and that is crucial when leading a team.

There is a world-renowned quote that sums up exactly what we are talking about here:

"Whatever your mind can conceive and believe, it can achieve."

It was written by Napoleon Hill in his 1937 book, *Think & Grow Rich*.

Leadership and management are the keystones of your business and any business is usually a direct reflection of its leader. This is like a mirror of what is going on inside their heads, both good and bad. As a Keystone, it is the rock - the foundation that holds everything else up. The main area is focussed on your ability to make good decisions, based on the information you receive and how you process it. Do you make snap decisions based on instinct or do you have a strategy and ask yourself questions first?

Questions like: -

- How much emotion comes into play here?
- How does the information fit in with your vision?
- How will you communicate it to your customers?

The way in which the brain works is something that unites us all. The left brain is the office and this is where the logical thinking happens. The right brain is the playground where your creativity runs free. The key to making good decisions is in getting both sides to work together as whole system. It is persuading those thoughts to orbit around the brain and be considered by both sides.

The human body analogy is perfect for business because both systems work best when all parts are aligned and running like a well-oiled machine.

2 - Management Sector

This sector is about the left brain – logic, writing plans, monitoring, and improving your business systems and regularly reviewing what is and isn't working. This is a lot like physical training; to build strength and definition, just as peak performance athletes do.

THE BODY

3 - Finance Sector

The torso: Just as our organs convert food into energy and waste, this is where a business processes incomings and outgoings. Our financial operations convert completed works into income and that into cashflow, which is the lifeblood. Without this, your business will surely die.

We all know that food keeps us alive, but if you want your body to work at optimal level you need good quality food. It's the same in business. Healthy eating, healthy practices. When you direct your focus toward gaining and working with those ideal clients, it will keep your business healthy. These are the type of clients who pay on time and work in harmony with your values. For your business to work at its best, you want to focus on attracting them.

THE LEGS

4 - Operations & 5 - Human Resources (HR)

These are the support systems of the body and the business. Here you want to focus on training, skills and power to carry your business forward. Aim to build legs like Mo Farah's because winning gold for him was no accident.

But Mo did not do it alone. He had a coach and together, they worked regularly and consistently to create systems. His coach trained him in a way that improved the odds of winning. He held him accountable and reviewed any, and all progress. That is exactly what we do for our clients.

Getting the right coach will make a world of difference to your business and this is not just for the rich and famous. It's true all successful people have coaches and mentors because they know how important these are and what an incredible difference they will make to their businesses. It will be the same for you if you find a coach or mentor with the right experience and who understands what you do. They will help you get the desired results.

There's a reason why kings, queens, presidents, athletes and businesspeople have coaches and mentors and that is one of the biggest reasons why they are where they are in life now.

When using the legs as a metaphor here, remember they will carry your business forward, so you need to train them into a strong and powerful support system that can run both sprints and marathons.

Too many businesses are just limping along because they didn't take the time to focus on and improve their Human Resources and Operations systems. For example, job descriptions, appraisals, performance management, recruitment and culture development are all things that can make a difference to the success of your business. Combine them with mapping out your entire customer journey to identify the pitfalls, plug the leaks and recognise ways to improve efficiency and that will give you the *WOW* factor in customer service.

Your operations must be clearly defined and working for all sides of the business, all the way from the delivery of the product to the final act of customer service. Make sure you have the right team in HR, as not having the right people in the right positions doing the right things is where you are most likely to fall down. When you get all this right, your team will be engaged and highly motivated in their roles.

The environment you create and the value and purpose associated with your culture is extremely important for your team. It is that which will keep them motivated and happy. Within your team is where you create leadership tiers.

Praising people when they are doing well may seem like a very small thing to you but to them it is big and makes a massive difference. It is a little like rewarding your legs with a nice hot bath after completing that marathon -

a) It feels good

b) On a practical level, it will prevent them from seizing up and keep them working efficiently the following day.

THE ARMS

6 - Marketing & 7 -Sales Sectors

Once you have built that solid platform to work on, you are ready to grow and the best way to do that, is with marketing and sales. These are the arms of your business and just like the arms on your body, they are stronger when working together. Climbing a mountain with two arms is no mean feat, so can you imagine climbing it with just one?

While using this analogy, think of them as hand gestures - welcoming your clients or grabbing new opportunities. And what about your existing customers; are you inviting them back with open arms, treating them like old friends and shaking their hands on a deal? Or have you not engaged with them after that first sale and they've been left feeling like a kid whose birthday you've forgotten? Failing to nurture your existing customers is a classic 101 mistake. To put this into perspective, did you know that it is around six to seven times more expensive to find new customers than it is to work at keep existing ones? FACT.

Look at the whole business as you would look at someone about to climb a mountain. During their ascent, they will be using their entire body to reach the top. They will need every breath, every step, every pull, push, twist and grab to get them there.

Building your business is just like climbing that mountain. If you want to reach the top, train like an athlete – It's that simple.

And that is exactly what the *Bright 7 Sector Model* is; a training system for your business and it will train you and coach you to reach the summit at the same time.

CLIENT SPOTLIGHT
Matt Spearman of ECO – Electrical Services

I first heard about Emerson on a telemarketing phone call. They told me Bright was doing a free business webinar for electrical contractors. This was during the pandemic when we all had a bit more time, so I had nothing to lose by attending. At that time, I was one of those electricians who had a lot of ideas but not the know-how to implement them and it sounded like the webinar could help me with that.

Within ten minutes of listening to it, I was thinking, *'yeah, he is talking about me here!'*

As I was scribbling down lots of questions, I realised Emerson was answering them before I'd even had the chance to ask! It was all really resonating with me, so at the end I asked what the next step was because I wanted to know how to reach my business goals and learn what could be achieved. There was a follow up call which I signed up for and from there, on to a strategy meeting. The results came quickly and for me, they were around mindset. Having been a one-man band; an electrician turned business owner, I'd since employed a few lads but had no real path to follow – basically, I was just making it up as I went along. But the minute I was shown what to do and had processes in place, I knew what we should be doing as a business and what we were going to do to grow. That mindset shift was massive for me and I figured out where I wanted to be in life, set my target and started working toward that goal.

Prior to working with Emerson, I'd been your typical electrician; on the tools all the time and working in my business, not on it. Learning that made sense to me and I knew then, I needed to spend my time in the office working on the systems to make everything work better and to make sure that everyone else knew what they were doing too. By doing that, if I went on holiday or was off for any reason, the business would still run smoothly.

During this coaching, Emerson recommended a book to me called 'The E Myth.' When I read that, it felt like the author was talking about me personally! It gave me a big lift and made me think - *I can do that*! Book recommendations were valuable to me and every time he recommended one, I'd read it and be geed up and looking forward to the next one. I also felt like that after our coaching sessions. But that wasn't all, there was also the mastermind; a group of like-minded tradesmen who you're able to bounce ideas off and help each other out. Each time we had a meeting I'd listen to how others had dealt with similar issues I'd been having, and it was inspiring. As the weeks went by, I found myself getting more confident and started contributing to the chat myself. This group were just different – people listened. They didn't talk over you and it was not full of ego, just men in the same boat as me, supporting each other with good advice.

Knowing you're not alone in something is also uplifting and it gave me a boost. We are a group made up of tradesmen, not businessmen. We're trained on tools not laptops and so, going through the 7-Sector System really opens your mind to a lot of things, if you're open to it.

I know, in the industry, it can be a bit laddish, and this stuff might be seen as something for fairies, but the reality is, you're running a business, so you must get out of that lad mindset. Down the pub, having a laugh and joke is fine but not all the time - not if you want to make a success of your business. It's time to be a real adult!

The Leadership and Operations modules were where it was at for us as without having the systems in place, we were going to fall flat on our faces.

For me personally, one of the biggest challenges was getting me away from a paper diary. I did it in stages – from a notepad to a *to do* list, then a smart sheet and calendar that is interlinked with my mobile phone. Now, we're completely paperless and all our engineers are on iPads too. They use the SimPRO software and all plans, instructions, quotes and invoicing run through it. There was a little bit of a kick back from some of the older guys who didn't want to use iPads but it didn't last long and they're all into it now.

I have to say it was all a bit strange for me in the beginning, as I'd been using a paper diary since back in the ark but it's great now and I don't know how I managed before. I can see clearly now, and I know what my vision is for the company. This has made a big difference to my time saving and headspace.

In the beginning, I spent a lot of time implementing everything and got very focused on that. Maybe a bit too focused to be honest, and I spent more time in my home office than I did in my home with my family. But putting in that effort has meant I no longer finish work at 10 pm each evening and miss out on family time. Now, I even share the school drop offs and pick-ups from the grandparents and I'm always home by 7:30 pm latest, so we get to eat and spend quality time together. That home office still gets used though, but now it's by my daughter who does her homework there.

At the main office, my team is much more organised and we've got more team alignment sessions coming up which work wonders. When I was spending most of my time on the tools, I often didn't get details of the upcoming jobs to my guys until the actual day of the job. They'd be just waiting around for my instructions; that was terrible time management on my part. Now, they look at their iPads and can see what they'll be doing in advance. One of the other benefits is, we no longer lose or waste time hunting around for drawings or paperwork because they are all on the iPad.

We can all see everything that's going on and just crack on with the jobs. My team are much happier now and there is absolutely no time wasting.

I've not been working on it long enough to analyse finance, but I know we were 200k down in turnover through the pandemic and, having run a quick check on the work we have done since, our profit percentage is up.

The mastermind I talked about earlier, is made up of all Emerson's clients, past and present and they all join in and give their time there. All of them have been through the business transformation journey themselves and are happy to share their success, so you know this works and you're also getting the benefit of all their learning too. Groups can be tricky but this one is welcoming and you don't feel like you're going to say the wrong thing or ask a silly question. You just feel at ease and everything feels achievable.

No-one wants to turn up week after week saying, 'no I didn't do it', so the accountability makes you get the work done! You don't want to let people down and why would anyone waste the opportunity when they've been given the tools to do it all.

Personally, I think it speaks volumes that the lads Emerson has worked with before, were all willing to come back into the mastermind and share their experience and advice.

There is an awful lot to be gained by working with Bright, and Emerson is easy to get along with. There is common ground between him and his audience and he is a 'trucks, tools, and tattoos' lad, not a suit who has just walked out of a high-powered office thinking he is *all that*. As a coach, he is down to earth and his approachability puts you at ease instantly.

'Leadership and learning are indispensable to each other.' - John F. Kennedy – 35th US President

2 LEADERSHIP
A Boss Has The Title A Leader Has The People

The subtitle of this chapter is quote from Simon Sinek and I think it fits perfectly with this chapter about leadership.

Now we're going to look at where you are at a basic level. Then we'll look at how you plan and move forward to a more sophisticated level of what you are doing now.

THE LEADERSHIP SECTOR

This is the first sector of *the 7 Sector Model,* and it is based on a five-level segmentation. You will notice that I use acronyms to help explain my processes and that's because they help the brain remember things more easily. So, for this leadership sector, I'm using the word UNITE.

The first and basic level of U.N.I.T.E. is U and it stands for UNIFY

Unification is the integration of *task* and *time* that then gets them to work together, not as individual things as many people see them. You may have both a task list in your note pad and a diary for instance but for them to work properly, within your best time management ability, the tasks could be taken from your list and added into your diary or calendar. In that way you are specifically allocating time to the task and blocking it out of your diary. By doing that, you're making that period of time unavailable for anything else, and it will give you that time to not only start the task but make sure you get it done too. It is the equivalent of turning your calendar into the kind of timetable we all used so efficiently at school.

GETTING ORGANISED – TASKS & TIME

To start getting organised in leadership, first look at task and time.

TASKS

There are two ways to describe this. The most common, twentieth century technique, is using a notebook. When you're in a meeting, you probably write a bunch of notes and maybe even add a bullet point or draw a circle around the most important tasks. When reviewing your notes later, you'll have many pages to trawl through and that not only eats into your time but makes it difficult to remember exactly what page you wrote them on, or even worse, which note pad you wrote things in because you use more than one. As a system, this isn't logical.

One way to avoid this kind of problem is to create an *action list* at the back of the notebook. That way you can flip straight to that after the meeting and then begin your tasks. If you're a real paper person, then get some focus sheets designed in an A4 pad. Use your daily priorities to plan the layout and fill in the sheet with your top three priorities for example and the most important task you must do the next day. When you've done that, leave it open on your desk for the next morning and that way, you can get right to it, and you won't faff around.

OK that's the twentieth century way but we're now in the twenty-first century, so it's time for an upgrade. As we're living in a digital world, we have many options for creating multi-listings and they can keep you on top of everything – you just must choose the one that works best for you. Some good examples are *Trello*, *Asana* and *Monday.com*, all of which are very popular. Personally, I use Microsoft *'To Do'* because when I researched it, I found that it was previously called 'Wonderlist' until Microsoft bought it and renamed it. Let's face it, they have the money to buy anything, so as they bought that one, it was probably pretty good! It integrates well for me with my other Microsoft outlook email and calendars too.

'To Do' has the option for multiple lists and this means you can chunk down as much as you like. I have one for each of my 7 sectors and I also have them for suppliers and my team. This is like having a shadow board to keep track of the tools in your workshop to know where they are when you need them.

One of the biggest time drains for a business owner is running around trying to find things!

TIME

In the twentieth century, most people organised their day in a hard copy diary. While that diary did the job, it did not do it in the best possible way. For example, let's say you slotted in a meeting for Wednesday at 2 pm and that meeting then got moved back an hour. You probably scribbled it out on the page and then rewrote it. But what if it got moved again, like it does all the time in the industry. After doing that a few times, you'd be looking at a scribbled mess and it would be hard to figure out what was what. At one time or another, this happens to everyone in business but there is only so much paper to use. The other thing with a hard copy diary, is that it's not backed up, so if you lost it, well, you'd be screwed. Not only that, but you can't share it with others so that you can all look at the same thing at the same time. And what about when you're on a job but you've left your diary in the van? That's where all your information will stay, until you get it back. Do you see what I'm getting at here?

In this twenty-first century, it is all about digital and using an electronic calendar. As a business owner, your calendar most likely runs from Monday to Sunday, with weekends open to negotiation (we all do it). This makes you mostly reactive because you're adding meetings and calls as they are arranged but if you were proactive, you would be better organised. For a start, you could add all your regular meetings, for example: - Monday's management meeting – Tuesday's training - Friday's finance meeting etc. You could also block out a regular chunk of time for yourself and use it to do your finances or something similar that you need to catch up with. Adding that in each week, such as every Wednesday between 2 and 4 pm, you're much more likely to get it done.

Make sure you block out the time in your calendar for the tasks that are a priority. The ones that need taking care of first. What this does is turn your calendar into a practical timetable.

Whatever you add in you're more likely to do but then what happens if it gets too full? Even before that happens, consider prioritising your workload.

To do that, break down your tasks into financial blocks like the ones below:

- £1,000 tasks
- £100 tasks
- £10 tasks

£1,000 tasks are the priority. These are the ones to spend YOUR time on because they will grow your business. Examples would be sales and recruitment hire for instance.

£100 tasks are important but not so important that you do them yourself. Many of these can be outsourced and that will free up your time. Bookkeeping and social media posting are ideal for this.

£10 tasks you should not be doing at all. They can be done by a PA, VA, or admin assistant. It is my VA who organises meetings and does the admin at Bright.

Looking at a full calendar can be overwhelming and often, that is when things don't get done. Adding blocks of time really helps because when you can see blank spaces, you know you have set aside time to catch up. You know you can get on top of things.

Ask yourself this: - did you ever have a meeting that bounced and you then used the time to catch up with your outstanding tasks? If so, I bet you got a lot done, didn't you? That is the same thing. That time can be used on whatever you want. It is both important and effective in catching up with your priority tasks.

By doing that, you've turned your calendar into something we are all familiar with … a timetable.

Think about it this way. No matter how many children there are in a school, it is the timetable that gets them to the right classes on the right day. It makes sure they learn the right lessons for their age group and get the right homework and it also makes sure they know what PE kit and what instrument they need to bring for what lesson.

A timetable is a super powerful time management system and the reason why it's been around for hundreds of years is because it works.

Start thinking about your calendar more like a timetable and schedule everything in it. Concentrate your time on the £1000 tasks and find a way to clear the rest of the stuff, by allocating it to members of your team. These are tasks you should not be spending your time on.

As the leader of your business, it is your job to grow and develop it and a timetable will help you do that faster and easier.

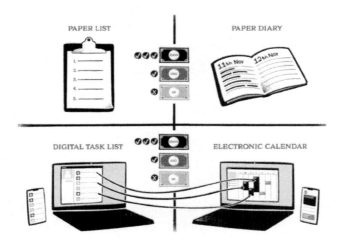

In a way, this is the soundtrack of your business. The beat of its music ticking away with a regular pattern in the background. These beats are the rhythm of your business, the heartbeats. The regular meetings that help your business grow. When they are set in place, you can add the reactive stuff that comes from client meetings and the general day to day.

Most of us have a long list of tasks which are often too many to fit into a diary. That's another reason why prioritising them is crucial to getting them done and done well.

To explain that better, let's look at rocks and sand.

You may have seen or heard this example before, but, as it's very appropriate, I'm going to use it here.

Look at the image above. An empty jar, some big rocks, some small rocks, and a pile of sand. Your job is to get them all into the jar.

In size, sand is the smallest, but if you filled the jar with that first, you wouldn't be able to get all the rocks in. But, if you added the big rocks, then the small rocks and poured the sand over the top, it would fill in any empty spaces without taking up the bulk of the room.

That is the same concept as your meetings and tasks.

The big rocks are £1000 tasks.

The smaller rocks are £100 tasks

The sand is your £10 tasks.

As I'm writing this, I know I've got a few videos to film and that is going to take a whole day of my time, so I've blocked out an entire day in my calendar. These videos are a top priority for me because by recording and getting them out there, it will lead to more business. But, if I'd filled my calendar with little tasks, I would not have been able to find a whole day to do the filming.

That is how you get things done … by getting them off your task list and *unifying* both task and time.

Taking your paper-based notebooks, diaries or calendars and transferring them onto a digital system, is a great way to get organised. These systems are built to make your life easier. Like I said earlier, I use a platform called 'To Do' because it works best for me. There are many other platforms, and they all exist to do the same thing … make it easier for you to manage your tasks.

There are many features in them, including the ability to integrate with your team. That means you can assign them tasks, send them notifications, and share folders with them at the click of a button. They are a game changer.

The second level of U.N.I.T.E. is N and it stands for NEXT

What do you want to do next? Where do you want your life to go? What is your vision? If you aren't clear about what you want and why you want it, you're not going to achieve it … simple.

This is about understanding what comes next for you and a simple way to do that is to use a vision board. It is something we do with our clients - getting them to create a picture that relates to the things they want to achieve in the future. Vision boarding is a visualisation technique, and we know visualisation works because it is one of the tools that top athletes use in preparation for competitions. For instance, these athletes visualise themselves winning gold at the Olympics before it's happened.

Have you tried visualisation before?

For it to work properly, you must fully focus on it; as they say, energy flows where attention goes and putting a vision board up where you can see it, helps you remain focussed on those goals.

To help you do this, we have developed a technique that works on your RAS - RETICULAR ACTIVATING SYSTEM. It is a system formed of nerves at the stem of your brain and one of the things it does is filters out excess information. Every single day, your brain receives a ton of data that the RAS sorts through to filter out the non-important things and offer up the bits that are important to you. The bits you've been focussing on. So, if you create a vision board and focus on it every day, your brain will learn to focus on these things and present more of them to you. But you must be careful, as this works on both positive and negative thinking.

A good way to explain it, is to look at some urban myths. I'm sure, like me, you will have heard many people say, '*it always rains on a bank holiday.*' That seems to be a commonly accepted truth BUT, it's not true. I know this because I tested it. Having heard people say it so many times, I started to pay attention to the weather on bank holidays and, as it turns out, many of them are nice and sunny.

It is simply just an example of collective belief; an opinion that has become fact. A fable if you like.

When you focus so much on a particular thing, that is what you will start to see. At some point, you may have bought a new car and then started noticing other cars that were the same everywhere. When my wife was pregnant, all I saw was pregnant women everywhere I went. This is a real thing. It's known as the Baader-Meinhof Phenomenon, and it's called *frequency illusion.*

This is something our brains do after noticing and paying attention to something for the first time. That then leads to you noticing that thing more often.

Ask yourself this - why is it that things always go wrong just as you're about to leave work on a Friday? If you looked at it and made notes, you'd see that this kind of thing happened on many other days too, not just Fridays. But as it is heralded as the end of the working week for most people, it becomes more noticeable because it's getting more consideration.

This is about paying attention and building a positive belief system around the things you focus on because what you spend your time thinking about is what you get. So, what next? What is it you're looking to achieve? Do take some time to create the next step in your business but first, work on what you want to achieve in life. Just don't make it harder for yourself than it should be.

A great tool to use is *The Wheel of Life* model. It focusses on three things:

- Health
- Wealth
- Happiness

Happiness comes from your relationships. Those with your partner, family, friends and especially yourself. It also comes from how you spend your time on hobbies and things you like to do. Take the time to think about your personal growth and legacy.

Health should always be your priority because what is the point of being the richest person in the graveyard? If you don't have your health, then you don't have anything. Sadly, most people neglect their health until it's too late and when they are diagnosed with an illness or disease, they wish they had treated themselves better.

The following quote sums it all up beautifully:

When asked what surprised him most about humanity, the Dalai Lama said, "*Man*. Because he sacrifices his health to make money. Then he sacrifices that money to recuperate his health. Then he is so anxious about the future that he does not enjoy the present; the result being that he does not live in the present or the future; he lives as if he is never going to die and then he dies having never really lived."

- Health is about you personally.

- Wealth is about what you have. Your working life, business, and career.

- Happiness, when you break it down, is all about your relationships with yourself and others.

A person on their deathbed never says, *"I wish I had stayed in the office and finished off those spreadsheets."*

They always say that the best experiences and things they look back on are what they shared with the people they cared about.

With that in mind, look at your personal interests. What things do you do now that you enjoy? And what about your personal growth and wanting to leave a legacy - what will that be?

If you start to look at all these pieces, you can create a wheel of life that can help you work toward and achieve the things you truly want. Statistically, it is the people with the most powerful and passionate visions who achieve their goals. Visualisation plays a big part in that.

For a long time, it was seen as *wishy washy* and then, science proved that it worked. The human brain fires up the same neurochemicals when physically doing something as it does just thinking about doing that thing. It's about conditioning your mind to be successful, and visualisation is a proven technique to help you achieve that.

Regarded as the greatest basketball player of all time, Michael Jordan swears by it. He has spoken publicly about it many times and said he used to see himself making the shots in some of his biggest moments that have turned out to be the biggest of the game.

Mo Farah also talks about it. He pictures success repeatedly in his mind and uses only positive thinking around it. That is not wishy washy.

At Bright, we use an exercise with our clients about living the dream life. You can do it too.

Look at your life five years from now. Where are you? What are you doing?

Who are you doing it with? Don't just think about this, write it down and create a story around all the things you want. Use all your senses as you describe it also. Using visual, auditory kinaesthetic, guttural, and olfactory references, breathe life into a story and make it easier for everyone to believe, including yourself.

Here is the one I used to tell myself:

"The sun was shining bright that September day, making it warmer than usual. Its golden rays warmed a patch of freshly cut grass and a breeze carried the scent in the air. I drove through the electric gates, the wheels of my new Aston crunching over gravel as I sighed happily. The kids were playing on their new trampoline, yelping with delight as they bounced up and down. My wife was walking across the lawn, carrying a bottle of Veuve Clicquot in one hand and two champagne flutes in the other. I parked then joined her on the garden swing. Popping the cork, I poured ice cold bubbles into glass, then, in gratitude, we celebrated how far we'd come from that two up two down in Milton Keynes - all the way to this beautiful country farmhouse. Exactly the kind we'd had in a photo that was pinned to the vision board we'd looked at every single day..."

That's not a fantasy by the way. It's my truth and we got there by visualisation and following my system. The only thing yet to come is the Aston, but I've written it in, so I know it is on its way.

You can do that too. Simply concentrate on what you want. Imagine it in detail and visualise it every day – don't just let it flicker in and out then give up. Think about it as if you'd already bought it and you are just waiting to move in. Put the images of all the things you want on your vision board, no matter what they are. Photos of a swimming pool. The mansion in the middle of the countryside. Your kids riding horses. The helicopter parked on the lawn (why not). You, standing on stage picking up a prestigious industry award. You, winning a ten-million-pound contract.

Think BIG because everything is achievable but only if they are things you really want. If you picture yourself marrying Angelina Jolie or Liz Hurley, then I'm sorry to burst your bubble … it's unlikely; but you can get a helicopter.

Breathe life into your vision and it will grow stronger every day. Tell the story to yourself, your family and kids and write it down in a journal. Write about it as if it had already happened and those things existed.

I am walking my vision right now. Sixteen years ago, we were living in a small, two-bedroom terraced house in Milton Keynes and now we live in the country at Hilly Farm. All those years ago I wrote a detailed explanation of this future and I read it aloud repeatedly - now I'm living in it. I wrote about it, talked about it, detailed it all the way down to the smallest elements and brought it to life in my mind. Then I worked toward it every day and eventually, it met me along the way.

You've got to feel yourself in that moment. What is it like? Who is there with you? What sounds can you hear and what can you see and smell? How are you feeling? Write a clear description about the future for your life and your RAS will create that filter and help you make it happen.

This is a great exercise that you can do alone, as a couple or as a family. Do it together and you have double the focus. Just make sure you are both on the same page and aiming toward the same goals. Get in alignment with each other and set the intentions for your life and your business.

I repeat, write it down because the weakest ink is still stronger than the strongest thought.

If you don't have a clear vision, it is like driving in fog. You will have to move slowly because you don't really know where you're going. You won't know what's ahead of you but, getting clarity will disperse the fog and you can drive off into the sunset and your destination, much faster.

The other thing is, if you don't know where you're going, how will you know when you get there? Get a crystal-clear definition of what it looks like in your future and keep that picture in your mind.

The third level of U.N.I.T.E. is I and it stands for INSIGHT

The greatest insights often come from the biggest knocks. These life lessons are necessary, but the road can be extremely long. The fact is, you will go much faster if you get a mentor or coach to show you the shortcuts. Working with a coach is like having a guide while crossing a minefield. You simply step in their footsteps to make it safely to the other side.

There are a bunch of tools you can use that will help you get the right information into your brain - the good quality stuffing. 'The sausage machine' is a great example and it is the creation of one of my friends, a renowned author and celebrity named Richard Wilkins. He is known in the entrepreneurial world as 'The Thought Engineer'. Richard says if you want to get the best kind of sausages out of the machine, you must put the best ingredients in.

That's not all though. You must protect the machine from any crap that could get in it. Nobody wants sausages filled with crap, do they? You must also be careful about this bit though, as it's everywhere - all around us. We live in a digital age, so it's hard to get away from all the crap and even if you don't read the newspaper, listen to the radio, or watch TV, you can still be bombarded with it from every corner of social media or the people around you who are reading, listening, and watching themselves.

Number one rule, don't listen to negative people who spout their opinions in conversation and rule number two, don't get caught up in clickbait and rubbish on the internet. You don't want those sausages either. Instead, feed your sausage machine mind with quality ingredients, like great audiobooks that can teach you how to be great. Listening to audiobooks is high on my list of things to do and I always recommend Audible to my clients. When I look at the best results and the biggest turnarounds, it is always from the clients who have been listening to those audiobook recommendations. Incidentally when you set up an Audible account you will get a free credit, so make sure you choose a book to give you plenty of insight and help you move forward in life.

Audio books are a great way to learn on the go. I've even got my thirteen-year-old son listening to them and I pay him for listening to books like 'Think & Grow Rich', 'Don't Sweat The Small Stuff' and 'Who Moved My Cheese'. At thirteen his brain can be greatly influenced, so I'm making sure he is learning skills that will help him in the future, instead of letting him just sit around playing computer games.

You can absorb a lot of information by listening and just imagine driving to work with Richard Branson in your passenger seat? How much could you learn on that journey? Can you imagine listening to him explain how he did what he did and giving you advise on what you can do to reach your goals?

Another book I recommend is 'Delivering Happiness' by Tony Hsieh. It is all about setting up culture and how to develop it in your company, along with the right team. If you've not heard of him, Tony Hsieh set up a company, grew it from zero and sold it ten years later for 1.2 billion dollars.

While I'm talking about books, I want to mention 'It's Your Ship' by D. Michael Abrashoff. For me, this book is associated with setting up your business systems. The crux story is about a Captain, who takes over a ship, knowing that he has a responsibility to improve systems and training performance. His job is to get the team to take ownership of their roles and become responsible, so that it is not all down to him. 'It's Your Ship' is a great read and I'd highly recommend it to any business owner.

The digital world is also full of podcasts and new ones are popping up every day. These too are a good way to gain valuable insight and, most of them won't cost you a penny to listen to. We're getting ready to launch our own podcast soon and it's going to be full of useful information for you to learn from. Check our website for more details about it and other helpful stuff that will help you build your business.

Don't forget actual books. Reading is the way we've learned for decades and if you don't want to buy a bunch of books, get a library card and read them for free. Books can change your life, just like this one will.

And so can people. Learn from those who have excelled in their lives and who are prepared to share their secrets with you. It's what I did when I first started coaching. I called all the coaches who were making waves at that time. I had no idea if they would help me or not, but I did it anyway. *Don't ask, don't get* as they say.

There's one last thing I want to mention – 'Blinkist'. There you can get a condensed version of the best non-fiction books around. The entire book is summarised in around ten minutes and, if you like what you hear, you can then get the full version. It's a type of *try before you buy* deal.

If you spend a lot of time on the road, why waste it? Make use of that time by listening to audiobooks from someone who can help you get where you want to go, faster than you could on your own.

There are other areas to look at when developing your knowledge. Masterclasses and online courses are examples and we run both at Bright Business Advice. I'm always learning myself and have been on many workshops. This has helped me learn how to do things using different elements and you can do this too.

Immerse yourself in live events and you will gain a lot. As you're attending, you've allocated that time to it and so you'll be able to soak up all the teaching with no distractions. Any kind of learning is valuable, whether it is in person, with a group or on your own, online. Each has their merits. You can even attend events that will challenge you out of your comfort zone, like a Tony Robbins event where you'll most likely end up walking over hot coals, bending bars with your throat or chopping wood with your bare hands. It's true … I've done it.

There's always something new and I hear the next big thing will be walking over broken glass. That's one I've not tried yet.

I'm a big fan of Mastermind groups and believe they are great for finding *your people*. If you've chosen the right one, you'll be mixing with people at a similar level to you and you'll be learning and bouncing ideas around. Whatever challenges you're facing, you can be sure someone else is in the same boat or has been there before you. That gives you a tremendous feeling of relief. With these, you will have both the understanding and the opportunity to learn from them because they have had the same experience and come out the other side. Brainstorming, solution finding and idea feedback are all things you will find in a mastermind group, along with those all-important accountabilities. Mine is called the Bright Mastermind Group and I run it along those lines. This really is one of my most favourite things to do; watching clients progress quickly and listening to them help and support each other makes me very proud. The format works like magic and not just in my group either. In my business capacity, I'm a member of a few masterminds that cover subjects like coaching, social media and webinars and I will continue to upgrade as I go because I practice what I preach. Why wouldn't I when I know it works?!

A mastermind is a hub of energy where ideas spark as you begin to grow and implement change because simply having the knowledge doesn't get you where you want to go. It is in taking action and putting what you learn into practice that gets you where you want to go and that is why I always recommend you get a coach or mentor. It is the 'fast track' and it will help you streamline and execute your ideas and boost your business in record time.

I see that in the same way as having a personal trainer. Mine is a guy called Del Wilson, a kettlebell European Gold Medal Champion. He is incredible and he pushes me harder than I would ever push myself. Don't get me wrong, I love kettlebell training and can easily lift the weights but Del gets the absolute best out of me because he knows how to. He knows what he is doing. That's what a good coach or mentor will do for you AND your business. Get the best out of you and it.

If you truly want to get to the next step in your business and you want to get there fast, you need insight from people who have done it themselves. That is how you speed up the process and get the fastest growth possible without making mistakes and wasting too much time.

As a client of mine Ricky O'Donnell loves to say: - *'Success leaves clues'.*

Talking of success. Let's look at one of Aesop's fables here. 'The North Wind and The Sun'

This is a story about a battle they had to see who was the strongest. They each took turns in trying to get a passer-by to take off his coat. The North Wind went first and blew hard, but that just made the man pull his coat tighter around him and hold onto it. The sun went next and simply shined bright. The man got warm, then warmer still and then he got too hot, so he took off his coat.

That analogy highlights the difference between a good leader and a bad one. The Sun here is emotionally intelligent and shows great skill in leadership by influencing others in this positive way. Acting in this manner will serve you far better than the outdated command and control style of leadership that was demonstrated by the North Wind.

Where do you need to put strategy in place? What type of thinking do you need? That may sound strange and you may be thinking, *well I just think!*' But this is about how you think things through and there are three types of thinking skills that we can all use:

- Analytical – Finding answers by using your memory or the resources around you

- Creative – Finding answers by contemplating unconventional or unorthodox means

- Critical – Finding answers using factual evidence or logic

The fourth level of U.N.I.T.E is T and it stands for TEAMWORK

A great team is raised by them having the discipline to do what needs to be done, while holding each other accountable. Your team must be trained properly so that they focus on the details and follow through on the actions. Working as a great team is easily demonstrated by the Oxford and Cambridge boat race. In each boat there are eight people who are being coached by a cox as they all work in unison with each other. I'm sure you've seen it on TV, if not in person. It is an image we know well. A team pulling together in synchronicity as they glide down the Thames. They make it look so easy, don't they? Of course, it's not, but with their skills and training, it is amazing to watch.

Who wouldn't want that kind of teamwork in their business? Get everyone working together like that, while each playing their individual part. Every single person is important and each one takes responsibility for their role. They trust each other and do what's needed when it's needed. With a team like that, you won't have to worry about a thing as you know the work is getting done.

With the right people in the right places doing the right things, you have a recipe for success and the more they *row* together, the stronger they will get as a team. This shows and grows discipline.

If you want to get ahead, create harmony. That comes from more than just the individual skill sets. It is from the team collaboration and the quality of their team*work* that will help you advance rapidly.

You already understand that kind of discipline because it's the kind we use when we brush our teeth every day. The regularity of it creates the discipline and, it's something you've been doing most of your life; a repetitive action that you're already an expert in. It's the same with business. Repeat actions daily to build discipline into your team and this will get them doing things right every time.

To create the discipline, you must have certain systems and boundaries and if someone falls outside of them by doing things that are not good for your business, it's down to you to keep them on track. That is where the accountability aspect comes in, with each person responsible for their own actions but holding each other accountable. Build a strong working culture of getting the job done. Grow the trust as people do what they say they are going to do. By following the systems and pulling together, everyone is in the same boat, rowing in the same direction, toward the same goal. It's called *SUCCESS*.

The fifth and most advanced level of U.N.I.T.E is E, and it stands for ENRICHMENT

When your business is doing great things and you have the time and money needed for your life, it is time for enrichment. At this stage, it's about reaching for higher levels in the wheel of life. It's about being part of something bigger and leaving a legacy you can be proud of. Another term for this is personal growth.

Look at Bill Gates, for instance. He certainly doesn't need more money, does he? No. The way he enriches his life is by getting out there and doing charitable work – he uses his wealth to do good.

What could you do to enrich your life? Here are some examples:

- Spend more quality time with your family
- Share your skills with your friends.
- Take time to evolve spiritually.
- Develop ways to support causes you care about.
- Find ways to give a leg up to people who deserve it.

Who could you support? What could you do to make your mark on the world and leave behind something worthwhile? Something that says you were here, and you did not waste your time.

Doing simple things like meditation or going for a walk in the park, is life enriching. Following your passions, playing sports, hanging out with good people are all ways to evolve as a human being. Or finding passions you didn't know you had, like taking up golf, trying a painting or sculpture class or learning to abseil.

Getting your time back is one of the biggest rewards anyone can get in life, especially as a contractor. This industry is renowned for that kind of working style but given the choice, you wouldn't work like that would you? When clients first come to us, that is one of the top things they talk about; not having as much time as they would like to spend with their family or on the things they want to do. One of them, who you'll hear about in this book, is Paul Gedney, a man who was totally time deficient when we first met. After going through our 7 Sector business model and working with us, he began living a completely different life. Most days, he has all his work done by midday and finds himself getting bored; can you imagine that? Recently, he called me in the middle of the day and as we were chatting, I mentioned how busy I was and he sighed, saying he had nothing to do. Hearing that gave me a flash of inspiration - a lightbulb moment as it were. Without any hesitation, I asked him to join us as a Bright Business Mentor. I knew he'd be brilliant at it as he'd already been through the 7 Sector system and had been a Brand Ambassador in the Mastermind Group – Paul was always supporting and helping new people when they joined. Now, he works for us a couple of afternoons a week, not because he needs the money but for life enrichment. He accepted the role because he wanted to give back to the industry and, he is really enjoying it.

We all have different ways of finding that enrichment and I found mine in becoming a trustee for a charity called Little Miracles; a charity that looks after children with disabilities and life limiting conditions. My clients have also supported them over the years by supporting me. Since Christmas 2020 and 2021 a couple of my Bright Advisors, Ian Mizon and Mike Sweet, along with clients Paul Gedney, Jamie Parsons, Doug Wady, and myself, have all rustled up teams, filled up our vans with gifts and dressed up as Santas to deliver presents to those children. This made me very proud of our Bright community and it is one of the most rewarding things we do. It is something we are looking forward to doing year after year, as we hope to go from local to national charity and as you can see below, we have created a tradition...

We could not go on without mentioning an amazing client of mine, John Davidson of Chiltern Cold Storage, who is in the heart of the pandemic as his business is in serving frozen food storage to airlines and restaurants. He managed to use the repurposed food in his warehouses to help us feed over 60,000 food parcels to families in need (figures true as of Dec 2021). John is the recipient of a Peterborough Civic Award, and he is a legend who needs to be praised for his amazingly good work for the Little Miracles Charity.

Contributing to the greater good will enrich your life in ways you never thought possible, just as it does mine. If you would like to help or support little miracles in any way, please go to www.littlemiraclescharity.org.uk

Here we've been talking about Leadership and to sum it up, it's about mindset. The way you think clarifies the direction you will take in life and business. It also determines your actions and ultimately, the results you will get.

'The key is in not spending time, but in investing it. Most of us spend too much time on what is urgent and not enough time on what is important. The challenge is not to manage time, but to manage ourselves.' - Stephen R. Covey

CLIENT SPOTLIGHT
Craig Winder of Winders Electrical Contractors

'We came across Bright just before lockdown hit. It was a post I'd seen on social media about a live event, so I went along as it resonated with me and I'd been thinking about getting a business coach for a while.

The first couple of months helped with the organisation side of things in the business and we got the calendars and internal organisation visible to all members of staff, so that everyone knew what they were doing.

I'd say the operations sector had the most effect on us. It was one of the areas where we needed the most support. I've been in the business a long time, so we were good with finance and some of the other things – we just needed an overall tidy up and to find a way to pull all the systems together to work better. That, and the accountability to get it all done, made a difference.

Going through the 7 sectors made me understand that I didn't need to do every job within the business myself or even micromanage it, so now I step back and the team gives me the reports. This has freed up a lot of my time and I'd say these days, I'm working 80% more on the business with 20% more time to do the important things, like picking my kids up from school.

The team feels much more valued, having been given responsibilities. They each have their tasks and get to control their areas while working within the system and to a deadline. Since we've been doing that, I've seen them step up a lot more than when I used to jump in and do it all myself.

When looking for help, I did look at other coaches, but Emerson works within the business with you. He doesn't just give you a list of things to do and walk away, leaving you to it till the following month. And I know if I call him, he is always available to give me advice.

The pandemic slowed things down for us but I can still see that doing this has put us in a position where we can grow, and the long term is looking good.

I would recommend Bright and I'd tell anyone to attend one of the webinars or speak to Emerson directly. Ask him about his business model and see if it suits what you're looking for. Being a coaching company that specialises in the industry, they are used to dealing with the same sort of problems we, as contractors, face. They've *been there and done that* as the saying goes.

Really, it's a brilliant model that he has set up and, if it's followed correctly, it will work for any business.

'A good coach can change a game. A great coach can change a life.' - John Robert Wooden - Considered as the greatest NCAA basketball head coach of all time.

3 PLANNING AND MANAGEMENT
Good Fortune Is What Happens When Opportunity Meets With Planning

That quote is from Thomas A. Edison, an inventor who developed many devices in fields such as electric power generation, mass communication, sound recording and motion pictures. That is a lot of lightbulb moments!

In this chapter, we are going to look at management by using the word P.L.A.N.S. as an acronym. This represents the five levels of sophistication on the Bright Orbit model, from basic to master.

The first and basic level of P.L.A.N.S. is P and it stands for PLANNING

Give your time, energy and effort to work **ON** your business and set aside the time to do so. When you do that, it will be easier to figure out what your next steps should be. This is about being proactive not reactive and instead of simply turning the spanners **IN** your business every day, you can work out exactly what you need to do and what you need to change.

As Henry Ford said, *'if you always do what you've always done, you'll always get what you've always got.'*

If you don't put the time aside to do this, you won't move forward in your business.

When developing a *real* business plan, the most important thing is to determine who does what by when. I say a *real* business plan because they are often seen as pretty pages that include a mission statement, a few nice flowchart images, and some financial graphs. They are the types of business plans people present to their bank when they want to apply for a loan. If you have one in that style, do yourself a favour and throw it in a drawer somewhere, as you will never need to use it again after reading this book.

A real plan is like a blueprint – the kind you would use on a construction site. It starts from the bottom up, with the foundation, then it ends as the real estate brochure to showcase the property in all its glory. These become the plans that are reviewed daily.

If you want a successful project, you must know where you're going, what you're doing next and what measurements and materials you need to build the next floor up. What components will you need after the shell? What fittings? First fix and second fix? How many? What size and how do they all fit together? What fixtures, finishings, and features and what about insulation? Just like a building, you build your business plan floor by floor, metaphorically speaking.

Then take it one step further. Make the plan active, so that it is continually evolving as life moves forward. That way you are prepared for it. This should resemble a blueprint that's been used so much it's grubby and wrinkled, with handwritten phone numbers written along the edges, wear lines in all the folds and bits of tape and Blu Tac still stuck to it, after the number of times it's been put up and taken down from the wall. It should look like this because it should be used constantly to develop and grow your business.

I personally use a piece of software that is a great planning tool. This is not only for my tasks, but it also allows me to go deeper into it all, as if I were mapping out a family tree - starting with great, great grandparents all the way down to the latest bundle of joy.

When you have everything down on that digital plan and you know WHO is doing WHAT and by WHEN, you'll be much better organised. After that, you can start planning the future.

There are three different levels of planning that involve short, medium and long term. To do this, we look at it like a pyramid.

- Short term – this is at the bottom of a triangle. A ninety-day plan that includes tasks you must get done. The twelve-month plan which includes yearly business goals

- Medium term – this is in the middle. The year after that, which includes milestones and indicators to show you that you're on track and moving in the right direction

- Long term – this is the pinnacle. The three-to-five-year vision. Where do you see yourself going, and what does it look like when you get there? Even if you're not one hundred percent sure of how you'll get there, you will know what direction you're going in.

This is programming your sat nav for a destination. While you're driving, you still need to know what's going on around you. That zebra crossing. The traffic lights. Those sneaky speed cameras. Congestion, accidents, and the inevitable jack-knifed lorries.

Start your journey with mirror, signal, manoeuvre, you then continue by pressing down on the accelerator and brakes, changing gears dependent on the road ahead and allowing extra time just in case you take a wrong turn. That way, if you do go wrong, you know you can circle back and get on the right road again because you have the sat nav programmed in. You have your map. All those things are happening in that single trip and yet, you drive effortlessly without consciously thinking about them, because you've learned to follow a system. You might be going from A to B but it's not just up the road to Tesco, it's all the way to France or Italy; the type of journey you prepare and plan for. A journey like this is not going to take you in a straight line and, without a map, it will be impossible.

That's why your business plan is both your map and your sat nav system.

The second level of P.L.A.N.S. is L and it stands for LONG TERM

Planning for the short term is always good because it takes you to the next step of your business but to plan for the long term, you must start thinking about the bigger picture. It helps to think about this in terms of a bow and arrow. The further you pull the string, the further your arrow is going to fly. Then you learn to control the tension and you can fire that arrow and hit the exact target you're aiming for.

In this section, we are talking about creating your longer-term vision and building on the excitement of where it could go and what it could look like. Think vision, values and purpose, all in this together. With a longer-term plan, we're talking about the next three to five years.

A really good book that I suggest reading (apart from this one), is called, 'Good to Great' by James C. Collins. It is full of brilliant content about your vision being the key thing that gets others excited about your business and where it's going.

At Bright, our longer-term plan is to help one million businesses world-wide. We want to coach ten thousand business leaders to create one thousand millionaire business owners, through one hundred coaches over the next ten years. Phew!

A big vision like that is sometimes called, 'a big hairy audacious goal.'

If we hit our goals, we're not going to stop and back up; we're going to carry on going. As Simon Sinek says, 'it's about being part of the infinite game.' That's also the title of his book, which is all about being *in it* for the long term.

It's important to keep going because your business is not just short term, is it? In the old way it was more about getting from one quarter to the next, with short term thinking. Doing it that way often leads to bad decisions being made because you're looking at the *day to day*, not the future. A better way is to think long term about your ethos, what you're trying to create and what direction you want to go in. Get that right and bring the right people on the journey with you. They are the ones who are excited to work with you and who want to be part of it because, when they feel part of something, they will put more effort and energy into it. Always choose them over those who are just in it for the payslip.

Your job here is to be the chief storyteller. Keep talking about your vision and get people excited to be on that journey with you.

The third level of P.L.A.N.S is A, and it stands for ANALYSIS

If you write a plan once, look it over with your team then put it in a drawer and leave it there, it is not going to help your business grow. That is why you review and analyse that plan monthly at a minimum. Take a good long look at it every ninety days, reset it for every quarter and keep your theme evolving, along with your business.

At Bright, we have a gigantic poster of our orbit that we stick *Post-it Notes* on. These are notes about key things we want to achieve in that quarter and by sticking them on the poster, the whole team can see where we are going and know what's coming up at the monthly review.

If you find that things are challenging or difficult, don't just read the plan every month – look at it weekly and see what needs tweaking. As a business owner, you should be looking at it all the time. Checking if you're on target and if you're not, how far will you go before pulling yourself back? Check all the things you're doing now and determine if they are part of that plan. If not, don't just let it ride, rethink it.

Ask yourself questions - What's the point of doing that? Is it the right thing to be doing? I personally have lots of ideas and projects that I'd love to do but I don't react to them straight away. Instead, I concentrate on what needs doing right now that will get me to a place in the future where I can work on those ideas and projects. These go into my plan which is there for the long term.

Some of my ideas are about creating software and others around creating global domination in the coaching world but I can't let myself run away with them. I must stay on track with my short-term goals if I want to get anywhere. To help with this, we have a weekly Monday morning meeting to review what we're doing. It works well and helps us stay on track, analyse results, and look at the numbers. This meeting is not just about analytics though, it's about questions too. The *why's* and the *what's*.

Why is that number high?

Why is that number low?

What are we looking at exactly?

What should we put into the report?

What do we need to look at that will help us recognise patterns and trends?

The devil is in the details, as they say.

The other reason we have regular meetings is to give us accountability. People make notes and have tasks assigned to them and those tasks have deadlines attached to them. It works well but when you put it in the plan, it solidifies the accountability because everyone knows who is responsible for getting it done and when the next meeting rolls around, they must report their progress. That is how the plan gets updated and why having the right people, in the right place, doing the right things, is so important.

Your confidence as a business owner increases when your people are going in the right direction. You can then step back and let them run it because they can follow the plan. This gives you the most valuable commodity of all ... *time.*

A client of mine has gone from working sixty plus hours a week and not having enough time to do all that he needed to do, to working ten to twenty hours a week, with plenty of time to walk his daughter to school. I've mentioned him already - Paul Gedney, who built his plan and his team, then stepped back and let them run it without him. If you don't have the right plan in place, it's not only your business that will suffer – it's you.

And don't forget, you must analyse the plan regularly or you just won't know if it's on target or not.

Interesting Fact:

Did you know that airplanes fly off course over ninety percent of the time? That is because it's impossible to fly in a straight line – this is all about course correction and that proves my point.

There may be times when it doesn't go to plan because of an act of God or a global pandemic and of course, these are circumstances you can't account for. In the unlikely event something like that happens, you may need to rip up your existing plan, change your ideas and steer your business in a different direction. I've been through it myself and had to completely pivot and as I mentioned, I went from running big events in hotels to hosting online webinars and zoom meetings. But I wanted my business to survive, so I just got on with it.

Use your plan to keep you moving forward and going in the right direction. Always know exactly where you are, in case, for whatever reason, things do not go according to plan.

The fourth level of P.L.A.N.S is N, and it stands for NOT *IN* BUT *ON*

Not in but on – That is what it is all about. Don't just go through the day-to-day motions working in your business. Instead, put at least twenty percent of your time each week into working on it. That's roughly one day a week and that ratio works well. Some of our clients take that whole day out of the office to work solely on their business from home.

Let's look again at a car analogy. A racing car this time. When you're in it, the time is spent mostly driving but to win the race, you must take regular pit stops for refuelling, topping up the oil, checking the tyres and changing any parts that need it. This is to improve performance and keep the machine in good condition, so that it can go the distance and not break down on you. When you're driving on the racetrack, that is when you're working *IN* it. As a hands-on business owner, it is very easy to get stuck on the tools, like an engineer or technician as is mentioned in the E-myth. In reality, the growth of a business comes from working *ON* it, like when you're in the office or managing the planning and systems development. You can also compare it to an entrepreneur taking a commercial view and having the vision to set the company direction.

Far too many business owners spend their time driving around the track repeatedly. They wonder why they are not making progress when they could be slowing down as things are breaking down and not being repaired.

If you want real growth and development in your business, take those ideas we talked about earlier and work on improvement. Use innovation and strategy to help you become a better leader. We've seen at first-hand, the results a client can get when taking the time to work on their business. It's like the pareto principle, otherwise known as the 80/20 rule. 20% of what you do will get you 80% of the results. So, what is your top 20%?

There's a book by Stephen Covey called the 'Seven Habits of Highly Effective People.' In it he describes the upper level as, *'working on the important but not urgent'*. That's why important things don't always get done because they are put on the back burner, while you focus on what is urgent. This is known as firefighting.

Block out the time to work on those things, instead of the day-to-day treadmill because it is so very important.

Imagine if you could swap things around here and work on your business 80% of the time, with only working 20% working in the business. Your business would absolutely catapult.

When you have one business up and running like this, you can create another or branch into different areas. It's like having an electrical contracting business then adding a mechanical arm and then perhaps a fire & security branch, as some of my most successful clients have done. Think about it in terms of a property portfolio. You start with a 'buy to let', then an 'HMO', then a holiday home or two, one here and one abroad. These are all things you can work toward making a reality and it all begins when you take the time to work **ON** your business and not **IN** it.

The fifth level of P.L.A.N.S is S, and it stands for SENIOR MANAGEMENT TEAM

When you build a senior management team, you are putting the pillars of leadership in place. This allows you to step out of the business and leave others to run it and it will run like clockwork without you being there if you plan it right.

Ultimately, you're looking for a senior management team in each element of each sector in the Bright Orbit.

The roles follow the structure below:

- Managing Director
- Operations Director
- Finance Director
- HR Director
- Marketing Director
- Sales Director

That is how a large business works. They have people in place who are prepared to step up and take responsibility for running and growing that business. For you to do it in a smaller sized business, all you have to do is mirror the structure.

You may find that when you're building a senior management team you must factor in extras, perhaps in the way of bonuses. This will give them more reasons to be involved – more skin in the game as it were. Nobody is ever going to care about your business as much as you do, so you need to find ways to connect the senior management team to the end goal. This will help them achieve results and work together as a team, not fight against each other.

If you can build a great team, with a great culture, you will have everyone supporting each other. Again, this is about having the right people, with the right skills in the right positions because then, your senior management team will support your business *and* the journey it's on.

What is very important is having your senior management in line with your culture and on board with where you want the business to go. Otherwise, they will water down the culture and your vision will change direction accordingly. Your team must buy into your culture, vision and direction which is why it's so important that they culturally fit those senior roles and are not just working in the positions based on their skill sets.

'The only thing worse than training your people and losing them is not training them and keeping them.'
– Zig Ziglar

CLIENT SPOTLIGHT
Danny Edmonds of Prowired

We were looking for a coach back in January 2021 when my business partner Nathan came across Emerson online. We then looked more into his business and we liked him because he looked like a normal guy - he'd been there, done it and worn the t-shirt. When we spoke to him, he was very clear about his system and he spoke our language, listened and understood the problems we were facing. After that initial session, we both agreed he was the one for us and right from the beginning, we saw results.

As a business, if we believe in something we will do it 110%, no messing around but if you do hit a problem, you need a solution. We're all human and so its normal to automatically think about the cost of doing these things but Emerson understood the problems and he offered the solution we wanted. His philosophy and outlook aligned with ours and we didn't disagree on a single thing. Out of everything we have done over the last seven months, not one thing has gone wrong. It's been absolutely fantastic for our business.

I now see things in a different light. As a person, I like things to work and I don't mind how much time I put in, to get them to do that. Some might say I'm a workaholic because of that.

We've been in business for nine years now and something we did from the offset, was to make sure we had a good brand design and image. We wanted clean and slick and that's what Emerson believes in too. You can see that from the whole Bright system.

I always go a million miles an hour, but I also have a young family - Olivia, Harry and my wife are the ones I work for. They are my life and I will work hard for them. With this system, I know I'm working towards spending more time with them and that's what it is about for me, so I've told myself that by Christmas, I'll calm down a bit. That is when I'll have been working with Bright for a whole year.

I'm an Electrician. I didn't train in business and there are no airs and graces about me but what I do understand is money and people. Now, with direction from Emerson, we've got that business training and it's all working fantastically.

We've installed SimPRO which normally takes seven months to install but with Emerson's guidance, we did it in four. I've also developed an app named PROWIRED which is available in the App Store. We're very proud of that.

Emerson speaks our language. There's no tech jargon or sales speak, he's a real, down to earth person. The other thing he does well is knowing which books we should read and learn from. Trust me, if he tells you to read something, do it and continue investing in yourself to give you more credibility. We've now been working with him over the last seven months and he has now gone from coach to friend.

Talking about books, he recommended 'Delivering Happiness', which is all about employing the right people for your business. Well, I read that book and decided we were going to test one of the ideas out. Out of all Bright's clients, we were the first to offer £1,000 to an employee to see if she really was the right person for the job.

Basically, this is a loyalty test to see if your employee is the right person for the job. Would she take the money and leave or rip up the cheque and stay?

We followed the whole recruitment process Emerson teaches and so we waved that offer under her nose to see if she would step up and show her commitment. I'm very happy to say she did rip that cheque up. Either way, it's a great safeguard because, if the money was too tempting and she walked, we would know she was not right for us. Yes, it was a gamble, but we were up for it because, we're in this for the long game.

Working on your business with Bright will make you aware of your surroundings. As a business owner it's easy to get blinded by the business and not see what is going on around you. The coaching makes you think about other people, how you treat them and how that affects the culture of your company. Before I had my own business, I remember working for a great company where I got on with everyone well but one day it all turned sour and it made me think. I'd never want that to happen in my own company. Never do I want to be so far up the food chain that I become unapproachable. In a work environment, it's great when everyone mingles as it's not only good for the people but for the business too.

With SimPRO, I can see what we're making on every single job and there's no doubt whatsoever that we are on our way to making more money. In business, you do have to spend money to make money and I know a lot of people are reluctant to do that because they are not sure it will work for them. BUT you won't get it until you've done it and when you've done it, you'll be singing Bright's praises, just like I am.

The other great thing about Bright, is the community. Emerson has a mastermind group that is helpful because you're surrounded by like-minded business owners, who are all trying to build and grow their businesses. Just last week, one of the guys had a job coming up in Kent that he couldn't get anyone for so we loaned him an electrician for a week. Now we've got a job coming soon up North and he is going to return the favour. That kind of support is really needed in business and it is invaluable.

If I had to sum our experience up in one line, I'd say that working with Bright is about getting honest constructive criticism you can work with and then develop to change your business for the better.

I just want to say full credit to Emerson for what he has built. It's a real success story.

'Numbers are of enormous help to anyone evaluating the worth of a business and tracking its progress. Charlie and I would be lost without these numbers: they invariably are the starting point for us in evaluating our own businesses and those of others. Managers and owners need to remember, however, that accounting is but an aid to business thinking, never a substitute for it.' - Warren Buffett

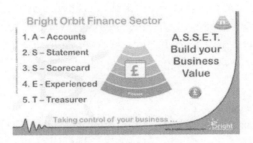

4 FINANCE
It Is Not Necessary To Do Extraordinary Things to Get Extraordinary Results

Legendary investor Warren Buffet first said the words above and I love it because I know it is true. I've seen it plenty of times with my clients.

We're going to talk finance in this chapter and of course, money is what keeps you in business. The financial sector in our Orbit Model is probably the most important part of your business. This is about making sure you are measuring the information and the data but more importantly, it's about making sure you are in profit. Business is about being in profit not loss and cashflow is the life blood of any business.

Not only do you need the right numbers you need to understand them yourself. Again, Warren Buffet tells it like it is with this quote:

Accounting is the language of business. If you can't speak the language, it's difficult to win the game.

You must have the right finance packages and make sure that your financial information is pulled together from all the different parts of your business. That data and information flow is best managed within the financial sector and it is crucial you get this right because too many businesses flop when there is a failure in their cashflow.

Statistics show that around 80% of all businesses fail in the first five years and a further 80% fail in the five years after that. Let's look at it like this; out of one hundred businesses that start up, only four of them make it to ten years. That is 96% failure rate and it's all down to the fact that most of them were not controlling their finances properly. It is critical that you get your finances right or you won't have a business at all.

According to statistics published in 2019 by the Small Business Administration (SBA), about **twenty percent** of business start-ups fail in the first year. About half succumb to business failure within five years. By year 10, only about 33% survive.

Over 90% of businesses fail because of cashflow
related problems

You can have the best service ever and make great sales but if you're not managing your money, that business will die. The financial section is designed to convert the cash that comes into your business from products and services, just like your body converts food into energy. This is represented by the torso in our *7 Sector Model*.

In the financial sector, the five-letter word I use to explain this is ASSET.

The first level of A.S.S.E.T. is A and it stands for ACCOUNTS

If you have a business, you need accounting information. Therefore, you must have an accounting system or platform to provide you with that information. I use a cloud-based accounting platform and I'd advise you to do the same. Xero or QuickBooks are very popular. Sage is really the system that started it all and that has evolved through the ages so you can also check that out to see if it's a good fit for your business.

The P&L is the profit and loss, which is like a history lesson, because you get the most out of it when you look back on it. It also allows you to measure the margins and see if you're really making money. That's the whole point of being in business isn't it. So, you need to determine if you're in profit or if you're making a loss.

When you start talking about *balance sheet profit line*, it's like an exploded view in the P&L. This shows you the workings and where they came from and is all about learning to read and understand the P&L statement.

P & L

INCOME	SALES A, B, C
COS	PARTS, EQUIPMENT, LABOUR, SUBCONTRACTORS ETC.

GROSS PROFIT

FIXED COST	RENT, RATES, WAGES, UTILITY, INSURANCE, VEHICLE ETC.

NET PROFIT

SALES %

To survive in business, you must be in profit. It's that simple. The P&L is also used to measure the margins and see where you can improve upon them by either reducing the costs or increasing your prices. What you're looking for is that sweet spot, where *the price is right*. I like to call it 'The Goldilocks Zone'.

If you find yourself having to give discounts, make sure there is a benefit to you from the client. It could be by negotiating better payment terms or asking for a longer-term contract which will help to improve your margins.

You need to know which customers are making you the margin so analyse the information and work out who your A and B grade clients are. These should be at the top of your list.

I designed a little grading code to help you here:

A = Awesome

B = Basic

C = Change

D = Delete

Ideally you want all your clients to step into the A & B categories but if they don't, it is best to change them for better ones or let them go and delete them. You can do that easily by putting your prices up.

FACT:

If you're too busy, it usually means you're not charging enough

As they say, don't be a busy fool. Put your prices up to speed control your business.

Don't forget the P&L is a history lesson and it's also like looking behind you - in the rear-view mirror. What it really is, when you get down to it, is a tool for the tax man which he uses to calculate how much tax you owe him. Literally, this is all about knowing how much tax to take from your business. That's all it is and it's why we must to do it. It's just a legal requirement.

It can be collated and adjudicated by your accountant, nine months after the year end. If you only see your P&L at that time, your accountant is not helping you because, by that time, the information is already eighteen months out of date. Make a note now to speak to your accountant about it, as you should be looking at your P&L each month at the very least.

This will tell you if you are on track and how much you have generated in sales income, so reviewing it regularly will ensure you're charging the right prices and know where you can raise them.

When people talk to me about charges, it seems they've made theirs up based on what other people are charging. The conversation goes a bit like this:

Them: *The average rate around here is X.*

Me: *Are you only delivering an average service around here then?*

Them: *NO!*

The fact is, you should be paid more if you're delivering more. Brand positioning helps and we will discuss that more in the marketing section. When you are in demand, you can raise your prices but if you are winning all the contracts, then you are priced too cheap.

Controlling your costs is all about managing the cost of sales (COS). This is the stuff you have on site like parts, labour, and equipment hire, etc. This is where you can improve the difference between sales - cost = gross profit.

Next, look at your fixed costs, minus everything that would fall out of your business if you turned it upside down and shook it. The rent, rates, insurance and wages (for non-direct site labour like admin & management). Keep your pencil sharp and aim to reduce those costs by 10% annually to drive down inflated costs.

This means your net profit is the gross profit - fixed costs = net profit

Use these figures to determine how much to save for the up-coming corporation tax bill and base it on how much net profit you are making.

A great accountant will help you look into the future by using a cashflow forecast. This is looking forward at your business through the front windscreen to make sure you can see what's coming at you. You do this to stay on track and avoid any crashes, just as do when you look both ways before pulling out at a junction.

By now you will know I love my car analogies. So here goes with another … The P&L is like looking in the rear-view mirror to see behind you - you're looking backward.

The cashflow forecast is looking through the front windscreen to see what is in front of you. That's you looking forward. This will show you what's coming up in terms of sales, when to expect money in and when you're due to make payments to suppliers etc.

It's the flow of your business and the P&L is something that most accountants can do for you, although most people who have businesses don't realise they need one.

Speaking to an accountant and getting a cashflow forecast is something I highly recommend.

Those clients of ours who had cashflow forecasts during difficult times, like the pandemic for instance, found it that much easier to manage their business and make good decisions about what they did. You will need this accounting information to do the same for you. Instead of making those gut instinct decisions, make them based on facts and information. That is crucial when dealing with the survival of your business or when helping it thrive.

Once you have your P&L, you can start analysing the previous month, the last quarter, the last year and so on to see how you have done. Then, look for trends and patterns. When reviewing historical information, the P&L is very useful, especially when looking at seasonal changes. That is how you spot those trends and learn to use them as a guide. Not only do we look at cashflow, but we also look for a twelve-week rolling cashflow to see what's happening over that period of time.

What I mean by a rolling 12-week cashflow is, that you shift it along every month by a month, so that you don't get to the end and fall off the cliff.

You will need to set a budget. This will allow you to understand how much you can allocate for things like marketing, new systems and anything else that will develop your business and help it grow. Set up a budget, assess the next twelve months and understand where you should be spending your money.

If you have a budget, this also drives you to negotiate harder when talking with suppliers. When they give you a price, you can counter with, *'It's got to be within budget'.* It's then down to them to meet your budget not the other way around. If you don't set one, they will charge you what they want because usually, when people in the business buy without care and attention, they don't seem to care about the price either it seems. Even if that is not the truth, that is the message being received by the supplier.

The second level in A.S.S.E.T. is S and it stands for STATEMENT

This is your financial statement that has the details of what you owe and what is owed to you. It is sometimes called a 'balance sheet'. You must know who owes you money and who you owe money to, as these are your assets and your liabilities. My question is, are you on top of collecting the monies outstanding? There are many businesses that get so busy, they don't get their invoicing done on time. If you don't get your invoices out in a timely fashion, people won't pay you in a timely fashion and when there's a big delay, you have a big cash gap. To close that gap, you must make sure you invoice on time. That way you won't waste time chasing payments and you won't have a gap.

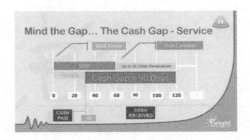

Look at your statement to see the age of the debts and who owes them. What process do you have in place for chasing them? And when you send those invoices, do you check they've been received? One of the biggest excuses around is, 'Oh I never received the invoice.' That's very similar to, "The cheque's in the post."

Whenever you send invoices, make sure you follow them up. Make sure the supplier got them and that you know their payment cycle. Do they pay at the end of the month or the last Friday of each month etc., It's important to know those details, then you will know when to expect your payments.

If you don't get paid, then it's time to bring out the chasing firm aka the debt collection agency. These guys are Rottweilers who stop at nothing to bring in your money. Ultimately, it's your money. Look at it this way, nobody walks into Tesco, picks up a load of shopping and walks out saying, '*I'll pay you later*'.

Managing supplier expectations is very important. When are you going to pay them and can you agree terms that give you some financial support? If you pick up bigger projects, because that's what it's all about, make sure you nurture a good relationship with suppliers just as you would any other partnership. If you do that, they will support you when you need it. Paying them on time is one way of doing that because when they know you as a reliable person, they'll know you're a good bet for better terms. It's wise to become known as a 'good payer'.

It's also important to have great stock control. Many business owners buy and keep too much extra stock on their shelves. They think that holding their money in stock makes them safer. But if the stock doesn't move, you will never realise the profit in it.

I had one client who built up a large stock to the value of £250k and he kept it topped up to supply a good client. But when he lost that client, he was left with the stock and had a tough time trying to sell it all on eBay. When this kind of thing happens, you're left selling goods for much less than they are worth just to get rid of them.

Be warned. Don't be fooled into putting your profits into too much stock. It is much better to use a delivery method and order in per job, then you won't have to sit on a lot of slow-moving goods.

It is also essential to build up the asset value of your business. This could be done through buying and owning buildings for example. You could also do it by building up the equity in the business, which is the money you have left over once all bills, taxes and dividends have been paid. If you want to build the value to sell it at some point in the future, then treat it the same as you would the housing market. Work on getting the equity value of your business to rise. This will ensure that a buyer will buy a solid business and you will exit with a bigger multiplier. Most business are roughly calculated as a multiple of profit (2-7 times) plus assets. The better organised, more profitable and solid your banked cash is, the higher multiple you can negotiate over.

The third level in A.S.S.E.T. is S and it stands for SCORECARD

These are your graphs, charts and statistics and this is where you can measure your business by information and numbers that go into a scorecard. The purpose of this is to know where you are at all times. If you turned up to a cricket match halfway through, unless you could see the score board, you'd have no idea what was going on in the match. Missing the first half would make it impossible to figure out what was happening but if you saw the scores, you'd know. There you'd see the overs, the number of runs, how many outs and how many wickets they'd had. Once you could see all that, you'd know who was winning.

Having a financial scorecard for your business helps you to look at its different areas and see how they are performing. Think of it like a car dashboard. The speed dial, the fuel gauge, the number of revs and warning lights - these are all indicators of the health of your car and, if you had this *at a glance* information about the health of your business, you would have something to aim for. It would also allow you to go for your personal bests (PB's).

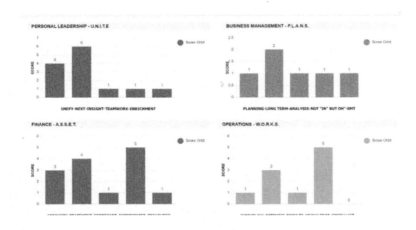

I keep a scorecard on my kettlebell lifting. I do this with my personal trainer and now we both know that I'm lifting longer and harder as I progress. Over the last few years, I've gone from lifting the twelve-kilogramme weight to the twenty-kilogramme weight and recently, I managed to lift that one for thirty minutes (it nearly killed me!) When I first started lifting, there was no way I could have done that but by measuring it on my scorecard, I know how I'm improving over time.

Keep a scorecard for your business and chart the progress, so that you can see how it's getting better. Analyse that information and the numbers because, as Warren Buffett says, 'the business cannot speak to you'. You can only talk in the language of business and that is numbers, so collect them on your scorecard and keep track of where you're at.

The fourth level in A.S.S.E.T. is E and it stands for EXPERIENCE

In other words, getting an experienced financial person on your team. You're looking for someone who just loves looking at spreadsheets. We all have different strengths and weaknesses and for some, numbers are a passion. Find one of those people who is really interested in them, and they will go into minute detail, looking at the margins, finding problems, looking for ratios and spotting potential errors, even before they happen. They enjoy looking over debts and suppliers and they will tell you what money is coming in and what the business can afford to spend. Plus, they will be aware of your budget and make sure that each department is keeping on target with theirs. This someone will totally manage your cashflow without breaking a sweat and they'll be excellent at dealing with the information in your business. Basically, they will keep on top of the P&L, act as the central point, be plugged into all things finance and be grateful for that too!

It is not necessarily those who have the qualifications in finance either. Those people are, of course, perfectly suited for the job, but experience goes a long way. Would you rather undergo an operation by a surgeon who performs the same operation ten times a day or one who got top marks in their studies on how it should be done? My point exactly.

Of course, the best person would have both qualifications and experience but do keep your options open and remember, it's all about the right people doing the right jobs.

You most likely know what it's like to work late into the night when trying to get all the figures and invoices done. That, plus trying to analyse what is happening in your business is a lot to concentrate on and getting the right support will make a world of difference to you and help drive your business forward.

One of our clients, Ben Donavan, had his wife helping him with finance but that wasn't her area of expertise and she really didn't enjoy the work. When she moved into a different position, he hired someone who was experienced in finance. This guy loved spreadsheets and he reviewed everything - checking all the credit notes, negotiating fixed costs with suppliers, getting the best quotes for insurance and utilities etc., and by doing this, he saved Ben's company a ton of money. He just loved the numbers, so he worked out all the figures and created a financial pack to manage the business better. It is incredible what can happen when you bring experience into your business and get the right people in the right jobs. This is a perfect example of how you benefit from having someone run accurate numbers.

The fifth and most advanced level of A.S.S.E.T is T, and it stands for TREASURER

This is your financial guru. Your FD. The person who looks at the numbers and understands them properly. This person can see the bigger picture, help you with complex tax issues and make sure you are completely legal and above board.

When we started with Paul Gedney, it was his wife who was doing the books for him, but his business was growing so fast that he needed to build that cashflow forecast. He decided to hire a temporary Finance Director who had all the knowledge and that person overhauled the entire system, putting everything in place. In the eighteen months we've been working with Paul (at the time of writing) he has now managed to retire his wife and she is very happy about that as now she can pursue her own passions and charity work.

If you have multiple sites, even across multiple countries, your FD is the one managing all the money and negotiating with banks for any terms around finance. They will manage a finance team under them if you have one and ensure you have all the financial data you need for your business. If you ask them how the business is doing, they will give you the correct information fast. It is the most sophisticated level of finance in the business and most small businesses don't get there until they're over ten to fifteen million or thereabouts. If you don't have an FD or a Financial Treasurer, it is possible to hire someone to do the job and you can get a high-level person from a company like the FD Centre (who have looked after a few of my clients when needed), for just one or two days a month. Either way, you want someone who will treasure your money, keep cash in your treasure chest and protect it at all costs. That way, your business will be stable, secure and in great shape to grow into the future.

One amazing bit of information I learned by reading a book called, 'Profit First For Contractors,' by Shawn Van Dyke, is that most people forget to include their own full wages in the P&L. That is often because an accountant has told them to take most of it out of the dividends, which comes after the net profit calculation. Accountants do say that is the most efficient way BUT, it's not the best thing to do for the health of your business. By doing it, you're not pricing jobs high enough to correctly include your own costs in P&L, as your wages are then ghosted across it. To calculate this properly, you must include your director's salary into the fixed costs, so that even if you take dividends from the net profit, after the P&L is calculated, at least you have included your costs into it.

To sum it up - *Bring in cash and retain customers for longer, as it is much more expensive to win new ones*

'It's what you say to yourself, about yourself when you are by yourself, that matters most.' - Brad Sugars

CLIENT SPOTLIGHT
James Parsons of Frontline Electrical

I first came across Emerson on LinkedIn, then in October 2019, we went along to one of his seminars and got introduced to him. To be honest, I've always been anti coach and had no intention of ever getting one. But I was very impressed with the progress of some other companies he'd been working with. I've now been with Bright ever since that seminar and Emerson has opened my eyes to the benefits of coaching.

We got motivated early on, right at the beginning of the system, and we were planning out our big goals. The strategies are so much better now and planning regular meetings in advance was a major part of that. Finance was another area that improved quickly. We'd always been good on figures, but we've now got a very robust cashflow system and that has helped massively. Getting the right people in the right places has certainly made a difference to us and our turnover has grown substantially; the system has 100% helped with all of that.

We've also adopted his love of books and the ones he recommended have really made an impact on us. Now, as a team, we all read a copy of the same book and sit down monthly to discuss the key points in it and, how we can implement them into our business.

Personally, I am much more motivated now. Before I'd been plodding along but I'm much more focussed these days and on top of monitoring it all. I just wish I'd started this years ago! Still, we're now in the middle of a transition period, putting down foundations and building on them to get the next level.

Emerson is a really good guy and we see him regularly. This has been on zoom during the pandemic, but I much prefer it in person as he brings great energy and we really get motivated from it.

The Bright system works, and I think it would work with any business, just maybe with a little adapting to suit the industry. I'd 100% recommend Bright (but not to our competitors!). Emerson is great to work with and the system is simple and easy once you've learned how. At the end of the day, if you don't understand it, then you shouldn't be a business owner.

Oh, and I think it's about time he took me for a pint...

'If it doesn't challenge you, it won't change you.' –
Fred DeVito – Author and co-founder of Exhale

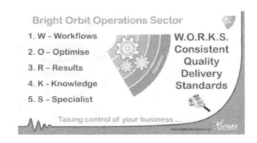

5 OPERATIONS
'Success isn't always about greatness. It's about consistency'

When I first came across that quote, I thought it would be from one of the great business minds but in fact, it's from Dwayne Johnson aka The Rock.

Now we're on the operations sector of the Bright system and this is about the work of the business and the products and services it delivers. That is why I use the word 'W.O.R.K.S' to break it all down and explain the best way to run operations successfully. Here we're making sure your business works effectively.

Whatever you do, whether it's a product or service, you want to make sure it works at an optimum level. To do this, you must manage the workflows across the business. It is the most important thing that clients want from you.

The first level of W.O.R.K.S. is W and it stands for WORKFLOWS

As a business owner, you must understand how your business works from beginning to end. Right from enticing the customer in, then through the entire process your business goes through until that customer comes out the other end. You want them to be happy with a fully installed job and their payments made on time and then your aftercare program kicks in. We call this 'the customer journey'.

Picture this as individual swimming lanes, it makes it easier to visualise. Simply name each lane with one of the following - Marketing, Surveys, Quotes & Estimates, Installation, Invoicing and Maintenance etc.

When we're working with our clients, we demonstrate this by laying it out in Post-It Notes as this helps them think about each step of the process and, what they need to do for it.

It also has its own easy explanation using the word F.L.E.X, as in *flexible*. This is to stress test your systems and make them work under pressure.

F = Flowchart

A good flowchart will show you exactly that - the flow through your business at a high level. This is easy to map out on a blank wall and you can do it with a bunch of coloured Post-It Notes! You can then convert it into a flowchart using Draw.io, Microsoft Visio or any software program that allows you to draw shapes into a flow chart.

L = List

Make a list of how each area of your business works. It does not have to be text only. You can include photos, videos or any combination of content that you want to create the "how to" manual for your business workflows and systems.

E = Engage

You know how it all works and your team need to get behind that too, so they need to be engaged by it. Make them feel part of it all and train them in the systems, processes and changes that are being made. When you're growing your business, involve your team because when they feel included, they grow in confidence and come up with ideas for improving the workflow. This is also because they are working in it every day and will often notice things you won't.

I once heard a great story about a man sweeping at the back of a room in NASA during a space race. At that time, the US President was visiting and he came across the man sweeping. He went up to him and asked, 'What are you doing sir?" The sweep looked at him then replied, "I'm putting a man on the moon." That is exactly what you want from your team. For them to get behind your vision and know that they are part of the journey.

X = X Factor

The X Factors are your WOW's. The things that make your customers say, 'wow, that's amazing.' To give you an example of that, I'll tell you about the hotel I stayed in on my honeymoon. They knew what they were doing and had their WOW'S perfectly planned in. Yes, there were all the regular things that hotels do, like towels arranged as swans on the bed and rose petals scattered around them for instance. And there were personalised trips around the island which included hidden gems or taking tea in residential huts, but the extras were things that didn't cost them a lot of money and those things delivered the extra mile. In particular, there were three great things I really appreciated:

We were served ice cold champagne at six o'clock every evening.

As we lay roasting on the beach, they brought out chilled towels that were vanilla scented.

And the last one was a WOW in capital letters. At one point, one of the waiters stood by me and lifted the sunglasses off my face. I thought *'you cheeky bugger!'* And I wasn't sure how to react, but when I looked at him, I saw that he had taken a cloth from his pocket and was now polishing those glasses. He held them up to the sunshine, checking for smears and satisfied there were none, he put them back on my face. That was very WOW worthy and it's one of the reasons I recommended the hotel to my friend as a honeymoon venue. That is how it works when you deliver a WOW.

It's the little touches that add to the experience and they live on in your memory. The X factor is something that stays in your memory.

Think about what you can do in your business that will create memories for your customers because if you can do that, it will turn them into repeat buyers who will do your marketing for you. Word of mouth is the best kind of marketing and advertising, spreading the word far and wide.

It will grow your reputation and your business without costing much at all.

This is also about consistency. If you get your operations right and the WOW's become part of your process, people will know what they're going to get when using your business and that is key in mapping out your workflow. Without consistency, the customer will never know what they will get and that can make them hesitant about hiring you.

The second level of W.O.R.K.S. is O and it stands for OPTIMISE

Once you've mapped out your flowchart, it's time to look for ways to optimise your business systems and improve the workflows.

Could there be a better software for you?

Does your phone system need upgrading to incorporate things like a call answering service? I had a client once without enough phonelines and when we diverted busy calls to an overflow, he picked up 30% more work in following three months! You can also use an auto attendant - you know the "press one for sales, two for support, three for accounts and 0 for reception, that type of thing. I know some people don't like them, but they are very useful and can efficiently route calls without bottle necking at reception.

Does your website need an overhaul to include pop ups, call backs or a live chat option?

Can you improve on team training?

Once you've mapped it all out, it's easier to optimise and move toward a 'Kaizen Process'. That is Japanese for a continuous and never-ending improvement - in other words, a change for the better, where you're constantly looking to improve. The great thing is, once you set a standard, you can keep raising it. That is what you want to do when optimising your business. Evolve the best service for your customers and they will flock to you because they can't believe how well you do it. Impress them and they really will want more of it and never forget that they will tell other people about it too.

The third level of W.O.R.K.S. is R and it stands for RESULTS

Ultimately, when you have clients and you want to get them great results, you must project manage that particular thing for them and make sure they're getting what they want. By managing the whole process and delivering results along the way, that is where the magic happens. It's an extension of having the right people, doing the right things, at the right time, which is what gives your clients the right service.

Designing a plan for the project and managing it to include WHO does WHAT by WHEN is what this is all about.

If the project is not complex and you're delivering a simple service, then over deliver. Make a point of getting the job done faster than expected. If it's a long process, make sure there is regular communication throughout and your client knows what is happening at every stage. That will make them happy and they will feel valued. This will also deepen their confidence in you and confirm they have made the right choice. You may have to train your people or they might have to learn new techniques for the project, so that they gain the necessary experience. Personally, I use a piece of software called 'Smart Sheet' for our customer business plans. It is built for project management and it's brilliant for making sure you manage the projects well. Within it you can add lists or Gantt charts together, while also seeing the process and systems you will need to get the job done.

Remember, this is all about getting results and the better your project management, the better those results will be.

Some of my clients are running projects on Monday.com, Trello or Smartsheet and they are getting great results. As I mentioned before, it is key to have the right people running your projects, as not only do they understand the importance of bringing the project in on time, but more importantly on budget. Otherwise, you could be better off not doing the work if it's losing you money. If you bring someone up from the tools to do the project management work, which is typical, then do make sure they get the training in project management too. You cannot just expect them to know how to do it. It's even possible to get them Prince II qualifications in project management and that is a well-recognised standard in the UK.

The fourth level of W.O.R.K.S. is K and it stands for KNOWLEDGE

This is about protecting the knowledge in your business. Are you backing up your computers into the cloud? Have you got emergency planning backup to protect the knowledge of the people in your business? How can you make sure the information in their heads remains in your business?

Many businesses, that have massive outage of data, fail in six months because they didn't have a proper backup system. If something should happen and you can't restore that information and knowledge, then you will lose it. Think about all the wisdom that has been built into your business. All the *how to* and *know how*. Backing it up means that you're organised; that your systems are technologically protected and that you're protecting the knowledge and IP of your business. Knowledge takes a long time to acquire but it can be lost in an instant if it's not protected. This is vital if you want to keep your business secure.

What disaster recovery requirements do you have in place? Who could have imagined the impact the covid pandemic would have on so many businesses? That has taken a lot of adjusting to home working with meetings by video, working with the kids and animals running around. It's been very different, yet we've all managed to do it.

I did have a client once who backed up his computers onto a hard disc. The problem was they left the hard disc in the computer room and then took it home at night. The lesson? Don't leave a hard disc in the computer room in case the server catches fire and burns the building down. Retrieving that data would then be almost impossible and it would cause major problems. So, I suggest you also lay out your disaster recovery plans.

What would happen in case of a flood, fire, power outage, internet outage or illness (even death). How would people continue to work at the office or even from home?

Another client of mine was once told that the building electricity was going to be off for two days. Luckily, they had a phone system, management software and database that was in the cloud, so they were able to camp out at the houses of the two directors and work from the dining room tables for two days and this continued their service delivery to customers as it was a twenty-four-hour call centre!

The fifth and most advanced level of W.O.R.K.S. is S and it stands for SPECIALIST

Have a specialist in charge. Someone who works specifically on operational organisation. It could be the operational director or manager but either way, it must be someone who knows how to make sure all the things you do as a business, are done well. This is then documented and managed across the whole business, and it takes the pressure off you. If you do that, someone else can make sure everything is coming in on time and on budget. This designated person can look after the systems and processes that make up the business operations.

It even includes things like the building you're working out of and the tools that allow people to do their jobs. All of this can be reported to you, so that you know your business is being properly managed and is working well. The beauty of that is, the hands-on taking care of it is not your responsibility. Having a specialist take care of these things, twenty-four hours a day, seven days a week, three hundred and sixty-five days a year, frees up your time for other things. Doesn't that sound great?

CLIENT SPOTLIGHT
Doug Wady of Wadys Electrical

I've been with Emerson since the beginning of Bright. All the way back to 2016 and we saw results with it straight away. When we had our first team alignment meeting, there was one guy who was dead against it all but by the end of it, he was buzzing. The whole team were, and the team spirit had entirely changed for the better. We spent a lot of time on the culture of the business, which was a new thing for us to talk about.

It wasn't just the systems and methods, but Emerson told us what books to read and he always had lots of ideas. As a taskmaster, he made us do things we might otherwise have put off until the following week … or the one after that! He held us accountable and kept us to our word, so if we said we were going to do something, we had to do it.

Some businesses may be scared because there is a lot of work to do and, it's not always easy to implement. There are books to read and software to get used to but what you get is the bigger picture and sharing this with the team makes it all doable. One of the things it did for us was give us confidence to go for bigger jobs with bigger contractors. We won lots of them too.

My biggest regret is that I didn't do this earlier in my career. If I were a younger man now in business, I'd bite his hand off for this coaching.

Financially, well, our turnover doubled. When we met Emerson, we had a target of ten million and were pulling in three million at that time. If it had not have been for covid, we would have made that ten million by now and he has helped us achieve that without a doubt.

Everyone has different ambitions and ours were wanting to grow AND have a great team who were happy in their roles. That is the important culture part of the business; it's about balance. Sure, you can chase the money, but we wanted sustainability because we're in this for the long haul.

If ever I'm at an event now, I watch those people on stage and I can see they have had coaching, especially some of our big customers who have billion-pound companies. I saw one of the chief execs on stage recently and he was talking about business – I watched him and could see clearly that he'd been coached. These people stay ahead of the curve and that is exactly what we are doing. If you're not doing it, you should be because it's what every business should do.

As a business, we implemented everything and had all the coaching and now we go back regularly for refreshers and to put our staff through leadership training. This helps us stay ahead of that curve and it's invaluable. You've got to keep your hand in and as for new ideas, well, they never run dry because Emerson always has fresh ones when we see him.

If you have a small firm, run by one person, your customers might get worried but now, with the whole team involved, this place will run without me. I can now retire whenever I'm ready and I'll be leaving a legacy behind. Like I say, I do wish I'd done it years ago and if there are any young'uns reading this, sign up and don't hesitate.

Emerson becomes like part of the team. A while back, he'd persuaded us to enter our first ever business awards and we won two awards, which was a great ego boost for us. They had yet to announce the main award but it was getting toward the end of the night and we were just having a drink and relaxing because we knew we were not going to win the big one. We were wrong though because they announced us as the winners. I couldn't believe it and there was Emerson, saying I should go up on the stage and make a speech. So, I did, and he came up there with us! We still laugh about that now. He was so excited for us. It was a total surprise and such good PR for our company that we started our own supplier awards after that and it's something we still do. That was all started by him.

'Technology is nothing. What is important is that you have faith in people, that they're basically good and smart and if you give them the tools, they'll do wonderful things with them.' - Steve Jobs

6 HUMAN RESOURCES
'You Don't Build A Business. You Build People and People Build The Business'

It was the legendary motivational speaker Zig Ziglar who gave us that quote. He was a man who truly understood how to motivate people and he knew how to get the best out of them, which is what we want to do from a HR perspective.

The HR Sector of the 7 Sector Orbit Model is like the other leg in our human body example of the 7 Sector Model and it's all about the people. You can have the best systems on the planet but if you don't have the right people running them, you don't have a business. HR is about getting the right people in the right seats on the bus and then going in the right direction … forward.

To start, ask yourself these questions:

- Are you maximising performance?

- Do you have a great culture?

- Are you making sure that your people are happy?

- Are those people engaged in their work and enjoying it?

- Do your people want to give their time, energy and effort to your business?

- Do they want to support you and help take your business where you want it to go?

If you've not said yes to the questions above, then that's something to work on.

Human resources are very important but often get left behind. When we look at our clients with the most successful businesses, we can see it is the ones who have nurtured the most powerful cultures and teams and they have understood the importance of HR. When looking at it from the body analogy, the right leg becomes operations and usually the most dominant part of the business. The left leg is HR and, in this analogy, it's like a right legged striker who is always scoring goals with that dominate leg. What this means is that they find it harder and less likely to use the left leg to score but we know, with training and practice, the left leg can be built up, giving them the confidence to use either to score. This maximises all opportunities, no matter where they are on the pitch or in the business.

It's all about trusting the team to take your business forward for you and allowing you to take more of a back seat.

In the Bright Business Advice methodology, we have a team alignment process that we ask our clients to go through with us and their employees. It works by making sure each team member is the right fit for the job and the company and they have the opportunity to share ideas on ways to improve the business in any way. After that, we work on cultural development of that team. This can throw up some interesting results and it certainly did for Paul Gedney. When he ran his team through the process, it raised a massive red flag with one of his main players. While you may think a main player would be the last person to raise a red flag over, it is something to be expected, no matter how long they have been with you. This is one of the benefits of the process as it will shine a light on something that ordinarily may have been missed. The purpose of the process is to help you develop the best possible team for your business and that must be done with total honesty. It's to ensure that the entire team are working toward the same goal, which is what will make your business a success. In Paul's case, the person in question decided to move on.

We had a something similar happen with another of our clients, Mark Brear. This time it was a client who was hindering his business instead of helping it move forward. So, picking the right cultural-fit clients to work with is also as important for the team. Identifying these things at the beginning of the relationship is important as it will make sure everybody involved feels like working together is rewarding and productive.

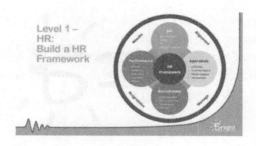

To explain the five levels of HR in this sector, I use the word HUMAN.

The first and basic level of H.U.M.A.N is H, and it stands for HR Framework

The elements of the HR framework are:

- JOB DESCRIPTION and ORG CHART
- APPRAISALS
- PERFOMANCE MANAGEMENT
- RECRUITMENT & INDUCTION

JOB DESCRIPTION

A job description brings clarity. It gives boundaries for them to work to. Your employees need to know what is expected of them. It is not just the skill set but also the attitude that is needed for them to win and be successful in their role and achieve the key performance indicators (KPI) so you can measure that they are doing well.

There should also be an organisation chart, like a family tree, that shows who fits in where, so that everyone knows the chain of command. This is best done as a visual and you can add employee photos to it. The chart shows who is responsible for what area and the allocation of their tasks and this is extremely useful for new employees as they can see how the organisation works overall and know who to ask questions when they are not sure what to do.

The basic policies are covered by a contract of employment and issuing a staff handbook as a guide is also useful. This acts as a form of guidance for all. I always advise that you have a competent HR consultant to help you create these. If done well, they will protect you but if done badly or not at all this can leave you open to tribunal issues from employees.

APPRAISALS

These individual evaluations are important, and I'd recommend that you do them regularly, at least every six months. It's common to do them once a year but that really isn't good enough – would you want to wait a year to help correct behaviour? The other thing I'd advise is a check in every quarter one to one. Maybe only fifteen-minutes will do, just to make sure everyone is on track.

During larger appraisals which usually last around an hour or so, you can analyse things like individual performance and your expectations, then decide on any training that person may need. You want everyone to walk out of an appraisal feeling happier than they went in. They should feel valued and rewarded, knowing that you really want them to succeed. Here you can use the burger technique if you do need to adjust any behaviours.

Good news, bad news, great news, or a sh*t sandwich as it is sometimes known in the trade!

PERFORMANCE MANAGEMENT

Performance management is the next step.

- How do you improve individual performance?

- What do you need to do regarding reward and recognition?

- How do you get people to perform at a higher level?

- What standards of performance can you use to measure accomplishments?

- How does your leadership team act and are they building emotional intelligence into your business to encourage higher performance?

Think about what comes at the end of the assessment. What type of recognition can you offer?

A certificate

A leader board placement

A real thank you

An award for employee of the month

We should never underestimate the value of please and thank you. It goes a long way and makes people feel appreciated, as does a regular pat on the back for a job well done. Taking the time to recognise what people are doing for your business leads to much happier people.

After that, it is all about the management. It could be that one of your team needs a performance improvement plan (PIP), to help them get back on track. This is the last stage before *'three strikes and you're out'*. If you're going to use this, it must be documented in your HR policy. It's important to speak to an HR consultant who can help you with company policy criteria and make sure you are covered. Using a PIP will also show the employee that you're prepared to give them every opportunity to step up. Any bad egg in your business will bring the people around them down and that is inevitable. My take on this is to let them go because it's better to have a hole in your business than an *'A'hole* in it.

If you have got the right people, they will perform right. If the performance level isn't up to scratch, then these people are not going to support your business. Fact.

Another of our clients had a team member move on after an appraisal that didn't go so well for him. Some time had passed and then one day, he popped into the office to say 'hello'. While he was there, he thanked our client because, after he had left, he'd found a job that he was so much better suited to and it was making him happy. That guy realised that he'd been in totally the wrong role for him before and that is one of the major benefits of stuff like this. It works for everyone. Some people hold onto jobs and some employers hold onto people for all the wrong reasons. Letting go opens the way for the right person to step into that space.

If there are problems with performance, it might be that your people are not in the right roles. If they are, do take the time to recognise and reward them. Celebrating their success is good performance management. This can happen at any level and could even be someone in a management position if they themselves are not being managed properly. Make sure you're checking in on everyone, no matter their role because they are all part of the team.

Recruitment and induction

To recruit the right people for the right jobs, you need a basic recruitment funnel in place to move them through an employment process. You do this in a similar way as you would attracting the right customers. Again, it's a process. If you're not an attractive looking business, you won't attract good quality candidates. You need to look the part. Think about it like this - If you were putting your business on a dating website, what would its profile be like?

Following the steps in this book is like doing just that. You won't just look the part you will *be* the part.

A good recruitment process is a bit like the old X Factor six chair challenge that is used to take a candidate up to the next level. This is a system where your potential employee makes their way through a series of levels, to prove they can do the job. It's basically a test.

Here is an example of the process and the levels/stages:

CV/Application form. This is the first point of contact you have with a potential employee.

Telephone interview: This gives you the opportunity to weed out the wrong people, so do make sure you have key questions prepared.

Group interview: This is time management. Interviewing in a group means you don't have to repeat yourself over and over again.

Application form: Now that you've whittled down to the best candidates, it's time for them to answer questions that are relevant to both the role and your business. Here you can go through the application from in more detail.

Presentations: When you've chosen the best candidates through the application form, invite them in to present themselves and, tell you why they are the best person for the job.

Final interview: Have another conversation. At this stage, the candidate should understand more about your company and how they best fit into it. Use a score sheet to justify your employment choices. If you don't do this, it leaves the way open to legal action if the potential employee feels they have been unjustly turned down for a role.

Trial run: When you've narrowed the list down to the best possible candidates, invite them in for a morning or afternoon and see who performs the best. You're looking for those who fit in with the existing team. This is also an ideal opportunity to get feedback from your team about the candidate too.

Check references: Don't wait too long to do this. It is a crucial element in the employment structure and should be done right at the beginning. You might instinctively think someone is just perfect and then you don't worry too much about waiting for their references to come back. A month later though, you might change your mind. This happened to one of my clients who didn't reference check until three months after employing a candidate. In the end he let that candidate go when his probation period finished, something that could have been avoided had the referencing been done earlier. Make this a part of your employment policy and it will automatically get done.

Through the induction process, your new employee will have learned a lot about the company and its culture, and you will have created the best environment for them and your team to perform at optimum level. Once they are in, the best way to acquaint them with the company is with an induction programme. I would recommend owner/senior manager checking in with the recruit pre induction (before joining) – Day one. Week one. Months one and three for example, so that they really know what is expected of them and will also feel important. It shows that you are interested in them. Don't just throw them the keys to a van and hand them job sheets to get done without first inducting them. Once properly inducted, they will know what is expected from the role and the culture and they will know the steps in how to do it as they go. All of this shows that you care and that they matter.

Talking about 'Delivering Happiness' again, the book by Zappos CEO Tony Hsieh, there's a section in it where he writes about offering a loyalty test to new employees - a $2,000 cheque. This is presented to them after their induction, and they are told they can take the money and leave or stay and keep their job and tear the cheque up. Sounds a bit of a gamble, doesn't it? But Tony believes if an employee turns the money down, they really want the job and will do their best in it. If they take the money and walk, well, he sees that as money well spent. That person, he says, would be wrong for the company and could cause more than $2,000 worth of damage to the business by staying with the wrong attitude or work ethic and it's most likely, you'd end up letting that person go. This is, effectively a 'no bad apples' safeguard. You will have read earlier that Danny from Prowired used this approach on one of his new employees and she tore the cheque up – it worked for him too!

I know I repeat this a lot but it's important, so I want to drum it in. Get the right people in the right places doing the right things. Induct them fully into your business and your culture.

As the chairman of Starbucks, Howard Schultz says, *investing in people is how we grow.*

The second level of H.U.M.A.N is U, and it stands for UNITY

Here we're making sure the culture is in unity with the team and the team are united by the leadership. Creating a business with a great culture is hugely important. It's about getting people behind your values and then all pulling together. If you attract people with great values and they all work together nicely, it is simply brilliant. This is like having a professional rowing team behind you and your vision, all using their united power to move you forward with a solid and consistent rhythm. That is the goal.

If you have an employee who doesn't quite fit the values or the team, even if they do a good job, they won't help drive your business forward. Instead, they become more like an anchor that weighs it down. This is another reason why your business culture is so important.

I talk a lot about Simon Sinek in this book, because he is brilliant when it comes to business culture, values and leadership. I recommend his books to everyone. '*Start With Why.* '*Leaders Eat Last,*' and '*The Infinite Game*' are all books to put on your list.

It's your business philosophy and principles we're talking about. The *why you do what you do* and how you choose to do it. Think about this in terms of politics. It is the mandates that attract the people who believe in the same things; it's why they vote. To this effect, your ideal team will believe in the same values as you and reach for the same goals.

Your business culture is your ten commandments. Here you collate your values and make them simple to follow. A great way to do this is by finding a word that embodies your business and makes it easy for people to remember your values. The word is then used as a memory hook.

Ours is BRIGHTER and it stands for:

B: Brighter futures

R: Relationship first

I: Innovation in all things

G: Growth mindset

H: Honesty always

T: Team Players

E: Engaging everybody

R: Resilient attitudes

Another client of ours, John Davidson of Chiltern Cold Storage, uses the word HUNGER as his memory hook. This is a brilliant fit for his business, which is in the food industry. It is used here in a positive way, and it stands for:

Honesty

Unity

Nurturing

Growth

Excellence

Respect

These can be used as a filter in the recruitment process and right from the beginning, you can start to measure how well people demonstrate your culture. Do they emulate or represent the values they are being measured against? Knowing the business culture will help employees meet expectations and it will also help you steer them in the right direction.

To measure the culture and engagement of your business, you can use a piece of software called, 'engagement multiplier', that runs staff surveys and collates the data for you. As I'm a partner with them, I can give you a free trial to try for your staff surveying. It gives you confidential and protected feedback from your team and it gives them the opportunity to let you know how they feel and express any ideas for improvements and confidentially. They can also highlight any areas they feel are a concern in the team, system or business leadership. It's such a good tool that provides great insight into your team and it's also something I use with clients as it is so insightful. If you pop over to our website and click on the partner page, you can register for a free trial. Simply scan the QR code and it will take you there.

https://www.brightbusinessadvice.com/book-resources/

It's not just your team that aligns with the business culture, it also spreads out to your customers. Many of them will buy into your business because they love the way you do business. This is because something about it aligns with their own values.

Take the time to think about all that and then think about what your word could be. What word would describe your business values accurately? Make it catchy so that you and your team will remember it easily and will know in an instant what your culture represents.

The culture of your business should never be underestimated. From that perspective, I was chatting to Paul Gedney recently and he mentioned that he believed it was the culture of his business that had got them all through the pandemic and held them together. His whole team had communicated well and supported each other, while also staying focussed. They had been prepared and ready to return to normal once the rules had relaxed. The team work so well on site together now and he has won more contracts than ever before and more than doubled the size of his business. Paul will say it's because of the power of the culture at RJ Wilson M&E.

Your business culture is powerful. It is the glue that holds the business together and allows you to scale it, by putting more of the right people into the business. Read 'Delivering Happiness' and you will see that Tony Hsieh, sold his company for $1.2 billion after ten years. This, he said, was down to having the right culture in place.

The better your culture, the better-quality person you will attract to your business, whether that's to work in it or buy from it. Fact.

Once you know what the culture is, don't just talk about it, show it. Develop your own acronym. Put it up on the noticeboard and all around the office or add it as the company screensaver. Refer to it daily like a mantra, until it's not just a word or a sign, it's a way of life. You can even use it and refer to it in your business meetings and appraisals. Drum it into everyone so that it just *is*. This is your business DNA and it shows everyone who you are and how you work. Ultimately it will give you massive results and create unity in your company because it's united by the leadership.

The third level of H.U.M.A.N is M, and it stands for MULTIPLY

We're talking about the multiplication of your business. This is when recruitment goes beyond the owner of the business. It's when managers and supervisors are involved in the process and it's no longer just your responsibility as the owner. This means more people and the exponential growth of your business, and that is why you need more team members to run it. Have a recruitment system to show how it works and developing managers can follow the process. You want to bring others into the business so that you don't have to make all the recruitment decisions. When you have the right people in place, they will take responsibility for the company recruitment and ensure they employ candidates who fit into the culture you've created. They will also make sure those candidates have the skills to deliver your products and services to the market, in a way your customers will resonate with. This means your responsibility will only be for the recruitment of senior management.

By multiplying your business properly, you will have set a recruitment process. That process is mapped out to determine how to take people from *interested* to *fully committed*. As we discussed in the HR chapter, you run candidates through a recruitment process in the HR framework, level one. As well as that, there are various things you can do to assess their suitability for the job. You can design a Q&A to score according to performance management or emotional intelligence systems and there are plenty of tools for that already. Personality profiling is a good thing to look into and a lot of those tools are free. For instance, Myers Briggs is a good one and it's very detailed.

These tests can be a great indication of who a person is at their core and what kind of role their personality is suitable for. Why not use these tests, because when hiring, the cost of getting it wrong can be very expensive for you. Recruitment is all about making sure that the multiplication happens first, then it starts growing by those tiers of leadership.

Find the right people and your business will grow. That is how small businesses become medium businesses become large businesses.

The fourth level of H.U.M.A.N is A, and it stands for ACHIEVEMENT

How do you create more performance achievement in the business? You can do this by having performance management across the whole of it. You may already do something like this with your sales team. Normally, these targets are measured, managed and rewarded by a bonus structure or commission of some kind but this doesn't have to apply for sales only; you can introduce incentives for all employees.

Profit shares work well. John Lewis does something similar, by giving all their employees shares in the company, effectively making them partners. A lot of businesses give shares to their senior management team as golden handcuffs, and this tends to keep them invested in the business and focussed on its growth and profitability.

If your employees can see there is career progression for them, they will work for it, but they also need to understand that working as part of a team will showcases their suitability for promotion. One of the best ways to bond a team is by bringing in a social element. Family fun days are popular, and I know clients of mine have given names like 'social squad' to this kind of thing and allowed for them in the budget. It is primarily to do with work, but the feeling around it crosses over and creates a sense of wanting to be involved, not having to be. This is when people start working toward a common goal and get a lot out of being part of a social team. It starts to feel more like a family.

Another engagement tool and performance improvement system can be found with a collaboration app called 'TEAM HOUSE POINTS'. Again, I have clients who use it, and it harks back to school days when there were team names and teams were given the opportunity to earn house points. You can use this kind of thing to reward each other for keeping to the culture and saying thank you to fellow team members. These house points or merits can be added up and converted into cash that the social squad can spend on fun activities – think bowling and pizza. There are lots of ways you can reinforce your culture and reward the team for sticking to it. You can download this app over on the partner page of our website as per QR code. This was used for an engagement multiplier to our partner page

https://www.brightbusinessadvice.com/book-resources/

You want your people to get behind performance and start improving and achieving. This is about being measured, being recognised and being celebrated. Create a business where the team want to prove how good they are and want to show their peers what a great job they're doing. Think about what achievement goals you can set for them to aim for.

The fifth and most advanced level of H.U.M.A.N. is N and it stands for NINJA

These days we think of a Ninja as a person who is expert or highly skilled in a specified field or activity. Although the Japanese the word *ninja* means 'spy'. Here though we are using it to describe the grand master in your team. Your HR ninja. This is the person who knows how to serve and protect you absolutely. They know everything about policy and procedure. They also know when to strike, when to defend and how to train your army of employees to get the best out of them. We all need a ninja.

This person will recruit the best people for you. They will also train and encourage them to be the best as they develop the team. Your business will become a people plant as more of them come in through the door and are nurtured to learn and grow toward greatness.

Great people do great things in your business. It's like creating an academy with learning and development programmes in place to improve the people. If you're not sure how to create an amazing environment for your employees, the ninja will know. They know that and so much more, but you don't see them in action. Everything just happens around you as the ninja stealthy and silently supports you. They make sure your team and your business are moving forward and being appreciated for it and you know your team is working together happily and are loving their environment. The culture is just right and the whole sector is safely being looked after by your HR ninja.

These people make sure your business works well and the rest of the team does too.

'Even though our core values guide us in everything we do, it is my fault we did not have values in the early years, because I thought it was a very 'corporate' thing to do. I only wish we had done it sooner!' - Tony Hsieh

CLIENT SPOTLIGHT
Ian Morris of I.M. Electrical

We started with Bright in January 2021 after doing something similar on a government scheme in London. I'd travelled down there every two weeks for one day of training. There I'd covered some of the subjects that Emerson teaches, but the problem was, I only half implemented some of the stuff because there was no-one giving me any accountability. We all know what that's like. You just don't get it done, do you. What I needed was someone to push us.

In December 2020, we started speaking to Emerson and joined one of his webinars. After that, we jumped in.

We've been at it for six months only, but we've definitely seen results, and from a personal point of view, I know where I'm going with it all. Before, I'd been left alone to steer myself along but I could only go so far under my own steam. My business dipped in turnover last year, I guess like a lot of businesses, and I just thought we'd get back up again by the end of this year but already we're almost back to square one and I know that's down to doing this with Bright. It all makes you feel like you're not alone and you have a rudder steer you forward.

Regarding the sectors, when we started we were already good at some of them and not so good at others, but our stumbling block has always been marketing. That's what we're working on now - dipping our toes in so to speak. It was this that was our weak spot — our gaping hole. Our business has been going a long time. We are profitable, with money behind us and good customers but there are always ways to improve a business, no matter what situation you're in.

Since signing up, I have more free time now and I know that in six months' time, I'll get where I'm aiming with the free time I want. This has made space and time for me to plan that in. I also had a good team behind me already and I've got my son as my number two and my daughter involved with the accounts. Now we're looking to expand and grow.

The thing with Emerson is that he specialises in our industry and that makes a massive difference. When I was on that other course, I found that in a room of fifty people, there was only one other person that was experienced in my area and we gravitated toward one another. The others there were doctors and accountants etc.

That was so different to being in the mastermind. There, I'm in a room full of people just like me who know this business. If anyone has a problem, you can guarantee one of the guys has the answer because they will have been there before you. It's a lively group and everyone has their opinions, but you always come away having learned something. The other benefit of it is that you just use the time you've got and hop in and out. Everyone understands because we are all busy and all in the same boat. We're contractors and that's the life.

As for Emerson personally, he is a really nice guy and he doesn't preach or push with a pointing finger. Down to earth and good at guiding you, he is always at the end of a message if I need something. There are times when I've been on another call when he has rung and left a message. When I pick up that pile of messages, he is always the first person I call back because that is his ethic too.

I would definitely recommend Bright to anyone. Especially for any mid-sized businesses in our industry who want to move forward.

'Always deliver more than expected.' - Larry Page –
Co-founder of GOOGLE

7 MARKETING
'You can't be heard if you're not communicating'

Simple advice there from Gary Vaynerchuck, a man with a net worth of around $200 million that he built on the back of the way he communicates with his audience. So, yeah, I'd say he was worth listening to.

Now we're going to discuss The Marketing Sector with marketing being the way you communicate who you are and what you have to offer the outside world. This is also carried over internally, as you use it to communicate with your team. I describe marketing as the right arm of our human body model and we are using it to describe the 7 Sector System.

The word I use to make the explanation easier is **LEADS**.

The first and basic level in L.E.A.D.S is L, and it stands for LEAD GENERATION

Ultimately, this is what marketing is all about - generating leads and opportunities for your business and getting a return on your investment.

Before you start, you will need a marketing plan and if you create an all singing all dancing plan, that has a lot of pages, it won't be easy to follow. It is far easier to have a single page only.

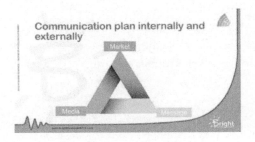

Market

First, determine who you want to target. You may have heard this called your 'target market', 'avatar', 'target audience' or 'persona' etc. If you know the details of this avatar, you will know how to market to them using language that speaks to them around what they do, when they do it, where they go, what they read and what their hobbies and interests are. The more you know about them, the easier they are to find and you can dig down deep into their psyche and create your marketing content to appeal to them specifically. If you're using b2b (business to business) marketing, it will be different to b2c (business to consumer) marketing, so it is crucial you know the difference.

Typical questions to answer:

B2C

- What age range do they fit into?
- Where do they live?
- What do they read or listen to?
- What kind of job do they do?
- What do they drive?
- What is their income range?
- How many children do they have?
- What problems keep them awake at night?

B2B

- What is their job?
- What industry are they in?
- Where is the business based?
- What online groups are they members of?
- What networking events or exhibitions do they attend?
- What magazines do they read?
- What challenges do they have?
- What stresses them out?

You get the idea.

Message

Start by answering the questions above and use that information to target your audience. You could also survey the best clients you've ever had, as they are the type of people you want to attract more of. Getting testimonials from those clients also gives you additional content to use and helps you figure out why some clients buy from you and not others. And, why they buy from others and not you. What is it exactly that your competitors service is doing differently than you?

When you know who your avatar is, you can start to drill down into your message. What do you say? Well, when you know what is important to them, it makes them easier to reach. Grab their attention in this crazy busy world we live in by speaking to them personally. A good way of doing that in your copywriting, is to use 'you' and 'your' style of language as if you are talking to them directly. Push their hot buttons so that they take action.

To connect with them, identify their fears, frustrations and desires. These are often called 'pain' or 'pleasure' points and it's about the emotion behind these points that you aim for in your messaging. You need to offer the solution to their problem, otherwise, why would they be interested?

So, what are the most common pain points of your customers normally? There will always be similarities between your clients, so think about what they have said to you when you've spoken to them about the job. Before you've quoted. What were their biggest concerns? Keep notes on all of that.

It is when people are worried, scared or wanting, that they most often take action. If you have a toothache, you go to the dentist. You will also go to the dentist for tooth whitening but that doesn't feel urgent, does it? But, if a dentist was right in front of you when you'd got that toothache, you would sit down in the chair wouldn't you?

That is why it is referred to as a *pain point* in any industry.

When researching your avatar, drill down into their pains when you create your message. Of course, you may have more than one avatar, so it's important to create unique messages for each of them.

When you talk to your audience in a language they use in their business, industry or life, it seems to them that you understand them and their problems at a deeper level. Say you were in a room with thirty people. Ten French, ten German and ten Spanish and you were trying to sell them something in English. How many do you think would buy? But, if you started speaking French to the French, German to the Germans and Spanish to the Spanish, you'd improve your chances wouldn't you. Marketing is just like that. Look out for it and you will see it a lot - someone shouting about their product or service in their own language, when the key is to tap into the language the avatar uses.

What is also important to remember is that there isn't a 'one size fits all'. Marketing is about specifics and people want to deal with specialists. If you were unwell, you could ask a pharmacist what medicine to take to make you better. But, given the choice, who would you ask? The pharmacist or a doctor? Most people would much rather take medical advice from a doctor because doctors have an expert understanding of the illness and training in how to heal it.

If you had a brain tumour you would want to see a brain surgeon, not a GP. Can you see where I'm going with all this?

Make sure your message is in the right language and that you use the right acronyms, tone of voice and terms in your marketplace, to show that you're the expert and a leader in your area.

Media

When you have really defined your message, it's time to look at media. Today that means online and offline. Where will you place your content? Where will it be seen by your customer avatar?

Whatever you're putting out there must look and feel like you, which is why your brand is so important. You want consistency of brand across all platforms, so that when someone sees it, they know it's yours. This is how you build brand reputation. Everyone knows the Virgin Brand of Richard Branson. It is red and has a logo we all recognise when we see it. You will see that logo on all their marketing too. The Virgin tone of voice and messaging is always a bit tongue in cheek too. When Richard Branson dips his toe into other markets, the competition worries because they do things so well.

At Bright, our brand ethos is built around this: Being passionate at helping business owners grow their own businesses, free up their time and give them the resource to enjoy that time with their families and friends.

You want your brand to be seen everywhere, both online and offline media and you want it to be heard with consistency and continuity of message. Ultimately, this is about making sure your message is in as many different places as you can get it so making it multi-touch. You'll also be driving that message at specific areas, to give you the best response.

Using a combination of different online and offline methods, how will you communicate to your different markets?

Online	Offline
• Website	• Exhibitions/ Events
• Google AdWords	• Newspaper, magazine articles or ads
• Email contact list	• Strategic partners
• LinkedIn – posts or direct messaging	• Direct mail letters / Postcards
• Facebook page, group or adverts	• Telephone calls
• Instagram	• Networking
• Clubhouse	• Customer referral schemes
• YouTube	• Flyers
• Webinars	• Seminars

Will you have a blog on your website? A YouTube channel for demonstration videos? Memes for Facebook advertising? Written articles in LinkedIn groups? Talks in Clubhouse? An email sequence of value-added information in a nurture campaign?

Knowing what each platform does will help you decide how to deliver your marketing content but what is most important, is knowing which one of these platforms your ideal clients hang out in.

Marketing has moved rapidly over the last ten years and the opportunity to be seen by more people is infinite. However, the competition for reaching them has also expanded, so there are more people vying for the same audience as you. Don't ever think that you might be overselling or saying too much because people don't see everything. That is impossible in the noisy world we now live in. What this does is further compound the need for targeting.

It's commonly accepted that it takes nine points of contact to turn someone from a viewer to a buyer but, due to the sheer amount of stuff out there, out of those nine bits of content, they may only see three of them. It means that on average, it will take around twenty-seven pieces of content for them to see nine. I learned that from Jay Conrad Levinson, the guerrilla marketer who also wrote the book 'Guerrilla Marketing'. Having also enrolled on his course, I learned from some very powerful content that he used unconventional and surprise interactions to promote products and services.

When you start marketing and plan out your lead generating messages, you will also have to capture contact data from your avatar. If you're using more than one lead magnet, make sure you verify where the leads are coming from, so that you know what's working and what isn't. You have an unlimited marketing budget if you can always show the return on investment from your marketing. If you could put £500 in a box and turn it into £5000, how many times would you put money in the box?

Did that customer come from an email, a phone call or an advert for instance? Use a reference or special non-geographic phone number to direct your viewer to a unique landing page or website. If you're ever in doubt, you can always ask them directly how they found you.

Data capture is mostly done by creating what is known as a 'lead magnet' or 'opt in'. You may have seen these online, as they are a modern-day form of advertising. Mostly, they are designed to give away free content in return for email details. For instance, the business gives you a free downloadable report in a subject you're interested in or watch a video and to get it, you have to fill in your details, which they then 'capture,' and use to market to you.

When designing a landing page or opt in, you create it specifically for your avatar. Use all you know about your demographic to create a marketing message that will appeal to them and offer something for free or at a discounted price. You then capture contact details, and they may very well turn into a potential client. On the sign-up form, you can ask for their name, address, contact phone number but the most important thing for online marketing purposes, is their email address. These details get loaded into your CRM (Customer Relationship Manager) database and you can use them repeatedly to market to that person unless they unsubscribe from your list.

People often forget that it is cheaper to market to an existing contact than it is to gain a new client. Going back to those same clients works out six to seven times cheaper than the money you'll spend trying to find new ones. Focus on your existing client base first.

If you've heard me speak before, you'll know I talk about a 'trust bridge.' This is about sharing contacts. Who do you know that can introduce you to new people? It's like you telling one of your contacts about me and putting us in touch. That person is taking your word for it that I can help them and that then gives me a certain credibility before I've even met them.

As an example, I was introduced to SimPRO software by a client who was already using the system. They had introduced me to the ECA who had recommended I attend the ELEX show and that is where I came across global brand, Schneider Electric. They then introduced me to the Professional Electrician Magazine and all those businesses have supported our Bright Business Summit events and introduced us to their customers. It is far more powerful to work on a referral (a friend of a friend or contact), than it is to work a cold lead picked up from a marketing campaign. The trust has already been established and it gets transferred by way of recommendation. There are many solid bridges you can build to take you from 'known' to 'as yet unknown' customers, but you will arrive with credibility if you've been recommended. Build these trust bridges with customers, suppliers, strategic partners and anyone else you can think of.

The second level in L.E.A.D.S is E, and it stands for ESCALATOR

At Bright, we talk about having a *value escalator,* which means at every step there is something available to the person who is ready to buy. Whether that is free, low cost, medium or premium doesn't matter. What matters is that there is something ready for them at all stages. But it also naturally moves them to ascend the escalator to higher value products over time. You want these people to go from *just looking* to *interested*, to *buyer* then *loyal customer* and finally, *brand advocate*. This journey may begin by them coming in at a low value item which they can test out and get an understanding of what you're like. If they like it and you, they may become regular customers and get to know you better. Eventually, they like you and what you stand for so much, that they want to promote what you do because they want you to do well. These are the people who become your brand advocates and raving fans.

There's a great book called 'Raving Fans' by Ken Blanchard and in it, he talks about taking your clients along this route. When you can do that, you will have people at the top end who absolutely love what you do, and they will tell others about you.

If you think about the big brands like Volkswagen, for example, their raving fans may have started with a small car like a Polo. As they progressed, they upgraded to a Golf, then a Scirocco and eventually to their first Audi all the way to the premium sports car the Audi R8 and so it goes on. That's what this is all about, making sure you have a product and service that helps deliver at every level of your customer journey.

The third level in L.E.A.D.S is A, and it stands for APPLICATIONS

When using apps for marketing, there are different ones to choose from, depending on what marketing you want to do. You will need a Customer Relationship Management System, which is called a CRM for short. There are quite a few around such as Mailchimp and Aweber and the more sophisticated like Active Campaign and Infusionsoft. I have used a few of these in the past but have now settled on Arkflux and QR code link to them can be seen on our partner page, as it allows me to make notes, track leads and move my audience though the different stages of the marketing funnel. It also sets contact reminders and automates email sequences to help me keep in touch and generally create a better relationship with my customers and prospect lists.

https://www.brightbusinessadvice.com/book-resources/

If you use scheduling software for social media posts, you can set posts for a specific time and date and this means you won't be wasting time creating posts in the moment. By scheduling, you can stack up content and automate the process. LinkedIn Sales Navigator allows you to build contact lists and connections and when those people take any kind of action on LinkedIn, it notifies you and you can take the opportunity to build a better relationship with them. A simple way to do this is by commenting on their posts for instance – Showing them you're interested in what they do.

You can also use a content management system such as 'ClickFunnels' to build your website and your sales funnels. My website is built on the 'Itseeze' platform and there, applications such as Arkflux, drive traffic and social media also. This automates my marketing and helps generate leads and it's all done on autopilot. Arkflux will also integrate into other software you have, for example, I know it's being integrated into SimPRO and this means you will be able to have front end lead generation and pipeline management, connecting to SimPRO for field service management of installations. That will link into your finance system and create a single flow of software and this will be brilliant for your automation and customer journey.

By using these software applications, you create marketing assets that you can rinse and repeat time and time again. Think about your video content for instance – one video can be repurposed into many other formats. The video itself, by stripping out the audio and turning it into a podcast, get it translated into copy, then edit it for a blog or article for social media. You can use clips from the video or stills that you add quotes to and turn into memes. The same applies to training materials. These can be turned into infographics that you can give as freebies on your website, getting viewers to download in exchange for their email addresses. Or you can use them as memes and give them away to your clients.

Think about what applications you are using in your marketing right now. Are you making the best use of the tools available to you? Are you collecting leads for your email database? This database is more commonly known as your *list,* and it is widely accepted to be the most critical asset you have. '*Your money is in the list*', is something you will hear loud and clear in most business and entrepreneurial circles. Do you know how big your list is? How many contacts you have in your database? It's important to know because that list is full of your potential clients – they have already had contact with you in some way, so there's no need for cold calling. These people are sitting there, waiting to help you make your fortune.

In today's world, that is one of the most common ways to market to your potential clients and, statistics show, that email marketing still gets great results (I know this to be true). Structured marketing to your list repeatedly will get you far better results than any other marketing you do. It is now about growing that contact list and nurturing those contacts because it will pay dividends over time.

Take the time to build your data list of contacts and make sure you use the right tools to work properly with it.

If you want to go deeper into marketing, I can highly recommend these books: - 'Marketing Made Simple' by Donald Miller and 'Influence' by Robert Cialdini.

The fourth level in L.E.A.D.S is D, and it stands for DOER

Everyone needs a Doer. This may be someone who is already in your team and likes marketing. Someone who is not just going to talk about it but will get it done by creating, writing and posting on social media. I have a marketing team who helps me and they do a variety of things, like updating our website, writing emails and creating landing pages. Basically, they do the work that needs to be done. There may already be someone in your world who likes this kind of work, and it may be a younger person as they have grown up with social media as a way of life. They will know a lot of things about it that you don't. If you can't find someone internally, you can hire an outsourcer and that doesn't need to cost a fortune as you can find many reputable outsourcers on places like 'Fiverr' and 'WeWork'. If possible though have a designated person 'in house' who has the knowledge, skills and commitment to your business to be a great team player and do the job well.

I would highly recommend you find some marketing doers, then you can focus on the most important aspects of your business - the £1000 tasks. Outsource the £100 tasks as much as possible and do that with ALL the £10 tasks. You focus on your job, which is to grow your client base, get the sales in and oversee the recruitment of key team members.

The fifth and most advance level in L.E.A.D.S is S, and it stands for SUPERSTAR

This person is the marketing genius in your business and it is their job to design the marketing plan. They can devise the strategies and tactics you will use to generate leads for your products and services. They will also know where to promote the marketing content, which will be carefully constructed pieces of content that have been created out of your business values. They contain the messages that will resonate with your avatar and communicate that you are the right people for them. Do include your suppliers and team in this, as that is what helps to keep your messages consistent. That person will manage your brand ethos and make sure everything is working correctly, including the leads that are being generated. Those high quality and low-cost leads that will give you a great return.

Normally, this person's title would be Marketing Director but, in my business, I like to call them our Marketing Superstar.

Great marketing is about finding the people who have a problem and need your solution.

CLIENT SPOTLIGHT
Dominic Gaziano of Drage Electrics

We started working with Emerson at Bright in January 2020, which was not long before covid hit. This meant we couldn't get started straight away. What we did instead, was use the time to implement all the systems and get our heads around it so that we could bed in. We did that over three months, then went to full staff in June. Then we grew a team internally by promoting the electricians who had been on the tools. They became our office-based estimators, project managers and office managers. Before that it was just me!

There were things we needed to invest in, like a new website and branding, but when you think that our turnover grew by 254%, it's been more than worth it. AND that's just in the 18months we've been working together.

Now we've got a management team I have a much better work-life balance. Well, I say better, I mean I have one! Before that it was just me 24/7 and even if I was on a break, I still had to be available. I was never truly away from work.

I had been contacted by coaches before and even since to be honest, but they have been generic business coaches. The thing with Emerson and his Bright adviser team, is that they really understand the industry, plus, he is now bringing in coaches who have 'been there and done that.' Those he has trained, who really know their stuff. A generic business coach is never going to get the same results as they don't really understand you or your business.

When you're working on your own, or with an untrained team, it's possible to get some success but you have to make many mistakes along the way - none of us has all the answers. It would have taken years to get to where we are now and I'd say, by working with Bright, we've done in just one year what it would have taken at least five to achieve. You can't put a price on that.

Don't get me wrong, I was sceptical and not 100% on board at first, but as soon as we got going, I could see the difference it was making straight away. Our initial strategy session was a total no brainer.

He's a persuasive bloke Emerson, so persuasive that he roped me into getting a home hair cut for charity during the first lockdown. He is on the board of a charity called 'Little Miracles' and when pandemic hit, their taps ran dry, so he set up a *Just Giving* page and ran a cut, colour, style or shave challenge. I think it raised around £3k in the end.

Of course, I agreed to it and my wife cut my hair. I don't think forgiven her yet, or him but with our net profit being up like it is, I just might...

'Approach each customer with the idea of helping him or her solve a problem or achieve a goal, not of selling a product or service.' - Brian Tracy

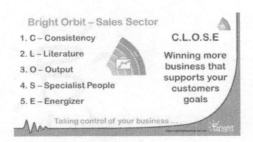

8 SALES
'Treat Objections As Requests For Further Information'

The owner of the quote above is Brian Tracy and he is the author of over eighty books. On the Global Guru list, he is ranked seventh best motivational speaker in the world, so I'd say he knows his stuff and I think his quote is really clever.

That all-important Sales Sector is always a biggie. I see it as the left arm of our human body model and use the word CLOSE, in association with our 7 Sector Model.

The first basic level in C.L.O.S.E is C, and it stands for CONSISTENCY

The biggest lack of sales comes from a lack of consistency as that is an important aspect in the sales process. This is about the way you handle a client and the way your team handles a client.

At Bright, we use a sales process that I have developed over the years from what I do now and the ten years I was in corporate sales. I call it our 'Rapid Sales Model.'

R.A.P.I.D is also an acronym:

R = Relationships. Building the right relationships with people who are in the sales cycle. They are not ready to buy yet but you're starting to build a relationship with them for when they are. We can look at this from a different perspective: - after a first day, you don't pop the question, do you? That is highly unlikely. Instead, you build a relationship with them first and sales is just that. It all starts with you building trust with them as a potential customer and they learn to believe in you and what you can do for them. If you want to sell to someone, you must spend time on them. 'Serve before you sell', as it were.

I know a lot of contractors who say they only get 'to do' tenders, so they don't get to build the relationships. However, you have to think about it differently. Think of a job you won – were you closer to them than the other guys in the bid? I bet you were. You probably got told where you had to be to win etc. They are helpful and responsive to your questions, and they are giving back, so actually, if all you are doing is tendering and not building relationships with the people who send you the tenders, you will probably be on a hiding to nothing and just used as a price check.

What are you going to do to build relationship earlier in the cycle? Can you be helpful? Could you be seen as a person to go to with questions and challenges way before they go to tender?

A = Ask. The way you dive into the fear, frustrations or desires of your potential customers, is to ask the right questions. That is so you can understand their problems in depth. What is it they are trying to solve? Do you have the right solution for them? If so, they will want to buy your service but first, you need to show them you understand. Take them from a place of pain to a place of pleasure and happiness by delivering your solution. Use open questions: What, Where, When, Why, Who and How?

Be interested not interesting.

P = Present. How will you present the solution? Will you put it in a format they want to look at? Is that a Word document or PowerPoint slideshow? Or will you explain it to them in a discussion after they have told you exactly what they want? Whichever way you decide to do it, you must make sure your solution meets both the problem and their needs. If you ask the right questions, you can get right down into the nitty gritty of those problems and that will help you get the sale. It is very important to present your solution in a way that meets their needs.

I like to use the concept of a 'doorframe' to explain marketing with the door representing sales.

It's about understanding your customers' needs and wants, their fears, frustrations and desires and about knowing your avatar from the marketing sector. In the sales sector, it is about finding and fitting the right door (product or service your customer wants or needs). From the sales process, you will know the size and shape of door they need to fit into the frame. So, when these match, the customer only needs to decide on the level of quality they want to buy. Plastic, glass or steal for example. When the door fits properly, you won't have to push hard to close it and if everything is in alignment, it should close with the slightest touch. This is also the case in a well manged sales process. The deal should close with a light touch and none of the old-fashioned heavy-handed techniques that door-to-door salesmen used back in the day. That gave salespeople a bad reputation.

I = Identify. Whenever you offer a solution to a customer, always give them three levels to choose from - the triplicate of sales. *Silver, Gold and Platinum.* In other words, economical, middle ground, and top end. By asking the client what solution suits them best for what they had in mind? You are giving them a feeling of choice and control and that works far better than trying to clinch a deal with just one solution.

D = Decision. Help your potential customer decide, then move them on to the next step. James Muir wrote a brilliant book around this subject called 'The Perfect Close.' He talks about if it makes sense to do 'X' for a next step as a close and explains it like this:

'If someone says 'no' to what you have in mind, ask them what a good next step for them would be. This is how you get *them* to decide and move along to that next step until eventually, they are ready to say 'yes'. Remember, you don't get married after a first date. You go through a relationship building process in which you get to know the other person in much more depth first. Only when you have done that are you ready for marriage and then, it seems like a totally natural next step.'

The Rapid Sales Model works. Just ask Paul Gedney who won three large clients in three months after completing it. Prior to that, he had been winning, on average, one new client every two years. Working through this system has more than doubled his turnover, which went from £2.5 million to over £5 million. You see, that is the power of the Rapid Sales Model and consistency is a big part of that. As you can see from Paul's story, not only does it work but it works very fast.

The second level in C.L.O.S.E is L, and it stands for LITERATURE

Having the right literature can really make your life easier when selling. Case studies of customer successes. Company profile documents, spec sheets and product information, are all the usual things that a business can create. These are all great and I agree, we need them to help smooth the sales process along.

However, a real point of difference that most people don't do, is design and build a sales model. This is like an explainer diagram in how you deliver the service that you provide. It is like the magic formula for how you do what you do, and it helps your customer understand what you do. This helps to create a visualisation instead of just trying to piece words together into a picture of what you do. If there is a proven formula, then your customers can understand it and most importantly, they can see you have one. If someone was trying to sell you a house, they could explain it to you but it would be much easier to understand when you are given the property details in a pack.

So you just need to review how you consistently deliver your service and create a model to explain it. Break it down and tell your client how it can help them. Create your own magic formula right now and it will massively improve your sales process and probably pick up a bunch more cross sells and upsells for you in the other things that you do.

Think about the 7 Sector Orbit you've been working through in this book. It is the kind of thing you want to replicate and tweak to suit your business.

Our Orbit is designed to demonstrate the model of how a business works. To get a copy of the 7 Sector Model and the contents of it that we use to help all our customers grow and develop, to achieve massive transformations in the results of their business, I've included a QR code below that will take you straight to more information.

https://www.brightbusinessadvice.com/book-resources/

When you design a company blueprint, make it one that can be downloaded from your website or sent as an attachment by email, perhaps as a PDF. You will also need a sales model to explain what it is you do. This is what we do with our Orbit model. Basically, it is letting a potential customer take a test drive so that they understand the power of what's under the hood. That document explains how your business can help them and that would be difficult to do if you don't have literature to back it up.

Think of it this way - when you're nailing something to the wall, you need a hammer. There is no point in trying to do it with a radiator key as it is totally the wrong tool. Using the right tools will help you nail that customer purchase and make sales so much easier.

The third level in C.L.O.S.E is O, and it stands for OUTPUT

Do you know what output you're measuring from the estimating/sales team? Is it results, in terms of actual cash output? Or is it the number of appointments made or the number of appointments that turn into sales for instance? This is often called the conversion rate. When you don't measure and monitor your targets, you will find that either your salespeople or your own sales will drop. That is why you must set goals and regular measuring standards and use them consistently, at least once a month. If you have a small business, it might be weekly or even daily. When you can gauge the output, you know what your salespeople are expected to deliver and when that gets measured regularly, you will either see improvements or lack of them. If someone is not getting the right results, HR needs to deal with that and find the right replacement to deliver. It is just business and you must have these things in place to drive your business forward. What are your Sales KPIs that drive up your output?

The fourth level in C.L.O.S.E is S, and it stands for SALESPEOPLE

As you expand your business it is important to have the right salespeople for you. Those capable of making and closing sales. You might call them 'estimators', 'contractors mangers' or 'project managers' and the title doesn't matter. What does matter is their ability to bring in new business and win new sales. Right now, it might be just you but as you grow, you can employ salespeople to expand the team and make your life easier.

I'm being brutally honest here about salespeople and I feel I have the right to, because I was one. So, have you ever heard the expression, *It's like herding cats*? Well, salespeople can be just like that. The great thing about it though is, when cats are hungry, they won't just come for food, they will hunt for it.

It is in your best interest to find out what makes your salespeople tick. What are they hungry for? You don't want the cool cat who is just cruising for snacks, you want the alley cat who knows how to sniff out top quality and is smart enough to close in on it. Find the hungry cats who look at sales like they would a fresh piece of salmon.

Your salespeople should not only be hungry they should care about delivering the best solutions for your customers. Trust me, the right salespeople will be a brilliant asset to your business.

The pushy type of salesperson is never good for your reputation and they are not good salespeople either. You don't want those *order takers, snake oil sellers* or *over promisers*. What you're looking for are the solution driven people who can show the customer your business has got what they need to buy. For your part, you must ensure they understand your business. Do this by providing them with documentation and the company literature they need to help them follow your sales process and generate more business. This is crucial.

The more they can help you serve, the more they will sell and the better everyone will be.

If you are paying commissions, always make sure they are on a gross profit margin and not turnover. Many poor salespeople will give it away if paid on turnover but as you know from the finance section, it is all about the margins. Encourage them to sell at higher margins with an incentivised commission scheme.

Salespeople are like athletes in that they need training and coaching regularly, to keep them sharp and on form. Also, they are competitive, so create leader boards to make sure they are striving to climb up. If they don't and are not interested, they might not be performing as well as they should do. Nurture reward and recognise your sales team but also don't hold onto under-performers either.

The cost of underperformance in sales is massive compared to the hitting targets and winning for your business, so be mindful of who is doing what, and monitoring their results is key to success.

The final letter of C.L.O.S.E is E, and it stands for Energiser

When you employ a sales director, their skillset should include being able to energise the sales team. You want someone who can rally a team to get them motivated and excited about going out there and selling your products & services. Being responsible for sales can be a difficult job sometimes and there is often a lot of negativities around it - I know, I've been there and I can tell you, when you hear a lot of people say no, it is demoralising. That is why you need an 'energiser' with the right personality to pick people up. This person can encourage others to get results and teach them the *how to*.

A great energiser will help others see, feel, and believe that they can do it themselves. If you can find this type of person, they will bring massive value to your business and, if you get the sales team right too, you're results will be truly amazing.

'Brand is just a perception and perception will match reality over time.' – Elon Musk

CLIENT SPOTLIGHT
Robin Hewit of RH Plumbing & Heating

It was 2020 when I started searching for business advice on Google. Bright Business came in as one of the top suggestions for the plumbing industry and that's where I first came across Emerson.

At that point, my business was not doing well. I'd also been offered a partnership that I was considering and I was just trying to figure out all my options. After I spoke to Emerson on the phone, we arranged a meeting and it was after that, I made the decision to keep my own business and put the Bright system in place. Since then, it's been a gradual process and bit by bit we're making the changes. I say *we* because I'm no longer a one-man band!

Around three months in, I hired a PA and everything felt like it was moving in the right direction. Now, I also have a right-hand man and some admin staff and I know I'm on the right track. Back when I started looking for help, I had a lot going on and I felt terribly pressured but there was no-one to share the load with me. It was a nightmare and to add to that, I couldn't sleep, even though I was exhausted from doing everything myself. Worry made sure I stayed wide awake.

These days it's all so different. I can delegate and my small team is really into the system too. They can see progression in the business and they know it's going to develop more which makes them proactive and they feel part of something bigger. My operations manager, Ryan, has been brilliant and as soon as he was given the opportunity, he became a massive part of the business and continues to work hard toward the goals.

Over the last year we've been putting the foundations in place, starting at level one and making sure we do everything properly. The systems and processes are making a big difference in the way things are run and managed. This was not necessarily easy to do but once you have it clear in your mind, it's easier to implement.

Before I signed up with Bright, I was talking to a company in London about a similar thing but to be honest, there was no comparison. They seemed more generic in their approach and they didn't speak my language like Emerson does. The coaches on his team have all been where I am now. That's why I know I just need to follow the process.

Because it's still relatively early, I don't know exactly how much by, but I do know we've increased our turnover and our team are pulling in more work, so I have seen the benefit already.

For anyone in the trade who needs help getting organised and laying down some structure, I'd say don't hesitate to work with Bright.

Having the group mastermind has been great and even though I've been busy, I've managed to squeeze in a session here and there and I'm always glad when I have. The guys are very supportive and I've even picked up work from them. It's funny how the smallest bits of information can make the biggest difference, isn't it? By doing this I got clear business direction and that was key because, at this time last year, I couldn't decide if I even wanted a business of my own … now look at me.

9 TOOLS & RESOURCES
Be So Good They Can't Ignore You

Here are links and information to tools and resources that will be useful to you and can be found on our book resources website pages. For free access to the resource page use the QR Code below.

✓ I recommend you download the 7 Sector Orbit Model to help you understand most of the content of this book. To help focus your own business growth journey.

✓ I also recommend you watch the short videos on each of the 7 sectors as I bring them to life for you.

✓ Lists of quotes from people I think are inspirational and really get you thinking.

✓ We will be adding more to the book resources pages all the time to include other useful tools and documents you can use to help build your business. And achieve Bright's goal to impact over 1,000,000 business owners' worldwide lives for the better by using the 7 Sector Model.

✓ We also will list our key partners who we mention in this book if you want to find out more about them for free demos, downloads and trials of their services.

https://www.brightbusinessadvice.com/book-resources/

Great quotes to remember:

'Good Fortune Is What Happens When Opportunity Meets With Planning'
- Thomas Edison

'It Is Not Necessary To Do Extraordinary Things to Get Extraordinary Results' - Warren Buffett

'You Don't Build A Business. You Build People And People Build The Business' - Zig Ziglar

'I Never Worry About Action But Only Inaction' - Winston Churchill

'People Spend Money Where And When They Feel Good' - Walt Disney

'Treat Objections As Requests For Further Information' - Brian Tracy

'Your Brand Is What Other People Say About You When You Are Not In The Room' - Jeff Bezos

'Be So Good They Can't Ignore You' - Steve Martin

'I was training to be an electrician. I suppose I got wired the wrong way somewhere along the line' - Elvis Presley.

'Your culture is your brand' – Tony Hsieh

'If people like you they will listen to you but if they trust you, they will do business with you' – Zig Ziglar

10 RESULTS
The Power of Implementing The 7 Sectors into Your Business

Here is a selection of our client testimonials – they are telling how it is in their own words...

Mark Brear – EML Electrical

'After working with Emerson for approximately a year we went from £150k - £750k in our second year to £750k - £1.7m. Next year we aim for over £2m. We have been able to implement structure into the business. From a management structure adding five people to the management team, employing the right staff to fit into the different levels within the business, through to introducing operational software with SimPRO that puts the process into the business. He pushed hard to get cashflow and finances under control and systemised, meaning we can make much better decisions about how we structure our growth, manage our margins, and pay myself a much better income than before. I have a virtual FD to help advise me too. In fact, I have totally changed my opinion on coaching and taking advice. Initially I thought it wasn't for me however, without the advice I think I may have really struggled.

From a personal point of view, the coaching and the books have absolutely changed my thinking for the better. Getting into personal development books has been a fundamental change in my mindset and it has been life changing.

I am no longer anywhere near the tools. Just office based and building the business. Doing the £1000hr tasks and delegating down all the £100 and £10 tasks to my team.

To make the business work better, we've introduced efficiencies and we have been able to improve quality and service that we deliver to the clients. We have now set the business up for a plan of strategic growth. We've also looked at our marketing strategy, through various forms of marketing and sales so can achieve the desired growth and this has resulted in growing the business tenfold under the support of Emerson from Bright Business. Seems like only recently we just won our first six figure project which we were really over the moon about and now we do it all the time.

We are building the team and now have over twenty people in it. Including apprentices and I am proud to say that we became a Finalist for the Apprentice award at the Peterborough Telegraph Business Awards in the Employer of the Year category.

I would say to anybody who is in this contracting industry and looking to improve their business, grow it or is seeking support for it, maybe discuss things with Emerson as he has a wealth of knowledge within this sector, as well as experience and a proven track record. He really knows what he's talking about!'

Ross Cawte – MD RJC Mechanical

'After starting a second business which had skyrocketed from £0 to £7m within 3 years, as the MD, I identified weaknesses within that business and embarked on the journey to take professional help. I worked with Emerson who helped me structure our business to ensure the staff were successful in their goals to help develop us into a leading M&E contractor.

Bright has not only helped to structure the business, develop goals and push the management to help us become an international contractor for government agencies, but to become a world leading export of the UK.

I would highly recommend them to any company who is serious in developing from a business of circumstance to business to be reckoned with.'

Ben Donavan – Jensen Fire & Security

'With Emerson's help from Bright, after attending his workshop, we put a plan together that has built the foundations for today's successful business growth.

Through coaching, we aligned the leadership team and got everybody taking the correct responsibilities for their roles. My wife, for example, left the finance role she was in and we hired a financial controller who loved the numbers and the details. Now our management figures are up to date and on time and that helps us make better decisions.

With Bright's help, we ran a team day that got everybody engaged and gave us loads of feedback and ideas from the team to improve our service delivery to get it spot on. This included quality checking planning meetings that were preinstalled to make sure everything would run smoothly.

I would highly recommend going through the Bright 7 Sectors with a Bright Adviser to show you what is working and what needs improving upon.

You'll get loads of ideas and accountability to get them done!'

JJ Electrical – Jim Brunton

'Watching the webinar was a light a lightbulb moment (pardon the pun). When speaking with Emerson, it was like everything was aimed specifically at me. We instantly knew this was the support and guidance we needed and from the initial strategy meeting, we were blown away with the knowledge and experience he brought to us. We are now in the early stages but feel so much clearer in our goals, thanks to the Bright team and the community of like-minded businesspeople.'

Leon Thompson – Safespark Electrical Services Ltd

'We first came across Bright Business Advice from a Facebook Advertisement, so we jumped on the free webinar, and hand on heart, it was one of the best decisions we've ever made.

Emerson has coached us to triple the size of our business in the space of just a few months.

He is very knowledgeable and knows business like the back of his hand and he is also very friendly and makes you feel comfortable from the off.

A truly valuable investment for our company and we plan to continue to grow and learn through the Bright Business Advice group.'

Oliver Whitehouse – Whitehouse Electrical

'I have worked with Bright Business Advice for 5 months now and it has been an interesting journey. It has given me a lot of focus and ideas to work on within the business and I'm now feeling like I've got the systems and the mental edge to move forward and grow the business in a more organised fashion, rather than how I have been working for the last ten years. As a business owner, you need someone to talk to, just to get things off your chest as it's a lonely place out there. So, if you feel like you're not getting anywhere, give them a shout.

Before I met Emerson, I was struggling for time for myself and my family. I was mostly working on the tools. Now, however I have backed off the tools and surprisingly, I'm not missed as much as I thought I would be!

Now my time is spent more on office-based work to generate and grow the business, which has given me more confidence in myself. We have worked on our tendering process and are now like a fine oiled machine, tendering for projects of over £100k! This year will be our highest turnover in 10 years, with the biggest profit and smallest outgoings.'

Doug Wady – Wadys Electrical

'I first started working with Emerson in 2009 when he was part of Action Coach and we did this for a few years, until we had a natural break in coaching. When Emerson set up Bright Business Advice, the timing was right for us to start coaching again and grow our business.

Although Emerson gave us the confidence to win larger contracts, increase turnover/profits, improve our processes & streamline our procedures, the biggest change has been in our culture.

One of the first things he did was a team alignment and from that day forward, we have had a huge amount of help from all our team. We have a business that was established in 1959 and staff retention was always above average but now everyone is more actively involved in everything we do, and I can't thank him enough.'

Robin Hewitt – RH Plumbing and Heating

'At RH Plumbing and Heating, we are a small firm with a team of 5, based in Bedford. We carry out all types of domestic plumbing, as well as offering commercial services.

When we first met Bright Business Advice and Emerson 12 months ago, we didn't have any systems in place to keep us organised. I was juggling working on the tools, as well as being a business owner.

Working with Emerson has taught us how to be more organised and how to implement so many processes. The most beneficial tool we have implemented is a job management software tool called 'Servicem8.' This allows us to quote, schedule and invoice a job from one app and it has also allowed us to manage the field team, as well as ensuring that we keep scheduling.

Most importantly, we now measure the profit on each job, allowing us to conduct our marketing effectively and ensure we are getting the jobs that give us the best ROI. Our team has grown and we now have a full-time project manager and admin personnel and this has helped us massively.

I would say to anyone looking at coaching for their business, it would benefit them tremendously to help get organised, systemise and prioritise.'

Duncan Grindley – Cambridge Electrical

'As a small company of four that is looking to expand, we were introduced to Emerson and Bright Business advice by the ECA, when they were running webinars during covid. I just felt there was maybe a good opportunity to try and change things within the business. As a business, owner things can get stale. I think you get a bit blinkered, and you just carry on doing the same things and sometimes, I feel it can be a little bit on your own, lonely at the top and you need a little bit of support. You need somebody looking from the outside to guide you in different directions and give you confidence.

During our sessions we changed a lot of ways we were doing things. I had ideas about wanting to improve the processes but never really got round to doing it and with Emerson's guidance and his links with some of the partners, it has allowed us to commit to things like SimPRO, allowed us to get rid of four different processes and four different apps, to put it all into one package.

As a company, we committed to attending monthly coaching and the masterminds. The mastermind meetings have been invaluable for our business and being in an open forum with like-minded businesspeople with similar problems, you feel that you can express and be open about everything. I think they feel the same and it is a great forum for new ideas.

My advice to anyone wanting to take this journey is, don't be afraid of criticism. We're probably all guilty of thinking we're always doing the right thing and being bosses, you don't get criticised because there's nobody there to tell you you're doing it wrong. To get involved with something like Bright Business Advice is good because they put you on the spot and make you accountable. Don't be afraid of it, commit to it and stick to what Emerson and the Bright Coaches teach. Follow the processes but most of all, enjoy the journey!'

Gareth Hughes – Multicraft Electrical Services Ltd

'We have been operating for 30 years as a business and have a team of 9 employees. We met Emerson after connecting on LinkedIn and watching one of his Manage, Control, Grow webinars.

I really liked the structured plan that he had set up and that's what first took us to Bright Business. We wanted to really address the issues we were facing as a business, such as employee engagement and plans for growth, marketing plans which we're still working on and still repairing good foundations.

We had a team session with Emerson which was good and that's really helped engage everyone and they seem very motivated at the minute. That is quite a fresh thing!

The benefits of working with Bright are that Emerson is very good at listening and helps you think and come up with ideas yourself. Ultimately, it is your business and he wants you to you know how to create it in your own eyes. He helps you clear your mind and come to these thoughts yourself, with a little bit of help.

If you're thinking about working on your business and you are short of time or struggling under pressure and you just want change in your business, Emerson is a great person to work with.

We also attend the monthly masterminds which are good because you end up in a group of peers. Everyone like yourself is running their business and you don't have that environment in your own business, so you must look further afield and that's where attending mastermind is unique. A group of likeminded business owners that will be happy to help each other out and that's a nice environment to help grow your business in.'

Matt Spearman – Eco-lectrical

'We are an electrical contracting company in Oxfordshire, with nine people working for us and we've been going since 2013 and working with Emerson since June 2020. In just over a year of working with Bright Business, we've taken on a fulltime administrator and moved into an actual office! We have built teams to make life a lot easier for myself and we've put systems in place like SimPRO, which allows us to quote, schedule and invoice jobs from just one app.

Before I started working with Bright Business, I was just an electrician with a business which I had lots of ideas about however, I'm not a businessman and it was hard to implement those ideas.

Since working with Emerson, he has introduced us to the 7-Sector Orbit and this has allowed us to focus on each of the sections such as, HR, Finance, Sales, Marketing, and Operations. The biggest area to work on for me personally was leadership.

For anyone that is struggling or wants to get more control and grow their contracting business I would highly recommend having a Strategy Session with Emerson, this will certainly help with your direction and implementation of strategies. The sessions also make you accountable, so you want to go back and ensure you have followed through, as you don't want to go back and say, 'I didn't bother' because you don't want to look like a wally!'

Danny Edmonds & Nathan Fibbrence – Prowired Electrical

'Five years ago, we moved our business to focus on industrial electrical works. We were first connected to Emerson through LinkedIn and then attended his Webinar at the end of 2020. The rest is history! We needed structure, we always knew we wanted to grow the business and be a certain size. We had a lot of things in place already, but possibly not at the right time, so Emerson taught us in a way that we could implement changes gradually to build the business how we wanted to. We employed the right type of people and started getting the right type of client as well, and we are working on getting the time back. We've made so many changes in a very short matter time, the results will come in for definite.

We also attend the Mastermind, which is good because there are times, as a contractor, you think you're on your own. With the support of the group, it helps to share ideas and problems to come up with solutions. If you're up for a change, Bright Business Advice will help your business.'

James Cufflin – Kibworth Electrical

'Having been coached by Emerson and Bright team for a year now, the difference I can see in my business in terms of structure and systems is night and day.

We now have a strong base to push the business onto the next level and clarity to see past mistakes we have made.

A bright partnership for the future'

Barbara Harland- Proklec Ltd

'Having started with Bright Business we are very impressed with the whole system. I have never felt more positive about growing our business, as it now seems we have the tools to keep us on track.'

Craig Winder – Winders Electrical

'I started working with Bright Business Advice just over two years ago now. The issue that we had before joining was an unstructured process and I wanted to smooth it out throughout the business.

The benefits I got from working with Bright Business Advice was to identify where the gaps were in our systems and discuss the processes and how to implement a new system that would make the process smoother. What I found was that Bright gave me, as a business, the time back from the upfront investment. I had time to do the things that I needed to do within the business efficiently rather than just reactively. Anyone looking to work with a business mentor? Then I think Bright Business is a fantastic opportunity for all contractors to identify areas of the businesses that can be improved.

I find the mastermind sessions are beneficial because they give the opportunity to work with other companies in the same sector, discuss the issues that we all have as a sector and learn what other companies are doing to smooth out that process for themselves.'

Tom Clarkson – Optimum Electric

'When we started with Bright, we were turning over 300k with 4 staff. We now have nine staff and are doing nearly 300k a quarter - a 400% increase!

We had a system in place for job management but working with Emerson has helped us to better manage our time and the running of those systems. We now have the right people doing the correct tasks for the pay level. We plan to improve our processes further.

We have moved into our own purpose-built unit and have space now to grow and scale up even more in the near future.'

Josh Bishop - Managing Director of EPM Engineering Supplies & Services

'Working with Bright since Nov 2019 and joining the mastermind and coaching I have continuously been proven wrong.

Initially my approach to development and change was that it was a negative and time-consuming process.

Throughout the sectors in the model of Marketing, HR, Operations, Finance, the improvement of Cashflow and Leadership, I have rapidly seen a change in myself which allowed me to become the businessman and entrepreneur that I always aspired to be. The only difference is that I am no longer happy with average. I am always using the Bright 7 sector model to continuously develop myself and challenge our processes to be better.

Becoming a member of the Bright mastermind – not only allowed me to change and develop but it showed me that the stress and disappointment I was placing on myself were completely normal and completely changeable with the right coaching and guidance.

Bright changed my business for the better but more importantly changed my personal life, giving me more time and money.

Even through a pandemic, we have made a new acquisition of a business, moved into a new property 5 times the size, upgraded our fleet, had a company rebrand, fully organised the stock, warehouse and computerised a 20-year-old paper heavy business and still made a genuine profit throughout a very difficult time in the pandemic in 2020.

Coaching for me is like the stone that makes a ripple on the water and it just keeps expanding out as you grow. Aside from the monetary improvements of the business. I've got the confidence to do more and not be afraid to be a leader. Dealing with my emotions, having the strength to make tough decisions and teaching me how to use the business tools I didn't even know existed, to build the business. Learning to appreciate the milestones. And appreciate the team. Fix the process and the person fixes the business. Selling their time and doing it with a smile on their face. I build the emotional bank accounts with the team through improving my leadership.

I have closed the cash gap. Put the clients in their place who now pay well and on time, we have processes to pick up the credit control issues. Been able to apply the learning to new clients coming on. I got the belief from learning to use the tools and getting the results and this gives me even more confidence spiralling it up.

My time management is better, block booking my time and now even finishing generally at 4pm every day. We got a management team together all with a completely new attitude and a Business Development manager to help me grow and he is smashing it.

Now moved into the office five times bigger and we've doubled the size of the team

Business grown 30% revenue and net; the actual profit has gone up by 30% too!

After the coaching, now in 2021 I have created a group of companies to prove specialist lubricants, installation engineering consumables and technical support and bespoke designed equipment and am looking to grow them all massively too.

If you can afford to join Bright don't let time be the decider, you will find the time when you get hooked on the results of the changes to your business and life.'

<u>Notes</u>

Remember the weakest ink is stronger than the strongest thought!

<u>Notes</u>

Key Action Task List

WHO	WHEN	WHAT

Products & Services offered by Bright Business Advice

Webinars

Discover how to manage, control, and grow your business to the next level by attending our FREE webinar on the 7-Sector Orbit

- ✓ how to quickly secure cash flow so that your business is always protected and has the resources needed to grow...
- ✓ how to ensure your workforce feels safe and motivated even in uncertain times...
- ✓ how to gain new customers regardless of what is happening to the economy...

We also have specific challenge webinars in our Bright Bite short sharp bite sized specific topic webinars thought the year.

https://www.brightbusinessadvice.com/how-we-help/webinars-workshops/

Workshops

Live in-person Business Accelerator Summits will be available as the world comes out of the pandemic and it feels like we are able to safely run them again. With support from partners, we will deliver powerful content based around the Bright 7 sector model.

Or you may wish to get some inhouse training for teams to improve your business performance including training on:

- Sales
- Marketing
- Customer Service
- Leadership & Management
- Emotional Intelligence
- HR for Non-HR managers
- Finance for Non-Finance managers

https://www.brightbusinessadvice.com/how-we-help/webinars-workshops/

Strategy & Business planning sessions

https://www.brightbusinessadvice.com/how-we-help/strategy-planning/

This is a must for anyone in business who wants to build a structured strategic business plan.

It's your opportunity to have a Certified Bright Business Advisor evaluate your business to identify and harness the many different areas of untapped potential, profits and performance in your team. This process is a vital first step in getting maximum value from your business.

You would never try and build a building without a set of plans yet so many business owners try and often fail to build a business without a set of plans...

The 3 hours Strategy Session is done using online video systems. To do this we take an in-depth look at your goals, both business and personal.

We map out a plan for you on our planning tool, so you have a stand-alone business plan ready to implement.

Masterminds and 121 business Advice & Coaching

How Masterminding works

You and each member of your Sector-Specific Mastermind group will benefit from focused brainstorming. We'll look at your specific challenges and you'll receive input from everyone in the group, including your Bright Business Advice experts. Online on video mainly and a several times a year in person face 2 face.

This isn't just a talking shop. You will leave each session with a set of actions to implement when you are back in your business. You will be accountable to every member of the group to get these things done. This is why Masterminding works so well.

Being accountable for implementing your goals drives you forwards, helping you to generate more profit and strengthen the structure of your business, building more resilience, accountability, and responsibility into your team. It will also help free up your time so you can focus on the future.

https://www.brightbusinessadvice.com/how-we-help/mastermind-groups/

121 Business Advice and coaching

Are you spending too much time working in the business rather than on it?

The team of business advisers and coaches at Bright Business Advice share their experience and expertise in targeted one to one business coaching sessions for 1 hr online on video and occasional face to face sessions if opportunity arises so that you can transform your business.

If you haven't had a business adviser or coach before it's a bit like having a personal trainer for your business. But instead of making your body fitter you'll make your business stronger.

Why work with a business adviser and coach?

Wherever you are in your business journey there will always be someone else who has more experience, skill, or knowledge.

Don't waste time and energy reinventing the lightbulb when there are people who are keen to help.

Directors of large companies have a board to support and advise them, but you're often on your own when you run a small or medium-sized business.

Making all the decisions yourself can be tough, so why not have another set of expert eyes look over your plans and another pair of ears to listen to your ideas?

Who uses business advice and coaching?

If you had a medical problem, you would see a doctor and you'd speak with your accountant if you wanted financial advice. As an athlete you wouldn't be taken seriously if you didn't have a coach.

Coaching improves performance when you're ready and willing to put in the work — it's just as true for your business as it is for elite sports people.

https://www.brightbusinessadvice.com/how-we-help/121-coaching/

ACKNOWLEDGEMENTS

To my wonderful wife Hannah who has supported me all the way through the highs and lows.

To our sons who inspire me to be a better man and a greater role model for them.

To my mentors Jon Bailey, George Hannides, Pam Featherstone and Zander Woodford-Smith, all of whom have helped inspire me to create the Bright 7 Sector system and focus on supporting the brave business owners who were willing to take the risk of building successful businesses.

Thank you.

ABOUT THE AUTHOR

Emerson Patton is the founder of Bright Business Advice, the only business advice company to be awarded ECA Commercial Associate membership and his coaching style has won him both national and global awards along the way. He has spent the last seventeen years helping three hundred plus clients increase their profitability, streamline their processes, and take back freedom from their contractor businesses.

These days he spends his spare time at home with his family in their rural farmhouse, a vision he worked hard to achieve but never gave up believing in. To keep fit he lifts kettlebells, practises martial arts and playing golf although, he is desperate to get back to the mountains for some snowboarding.

This is his first book but there are more in the pipeline, as Emerson knows he has created a winning formular that will help many business owners in other industries too.

Printed in Great Britain
by Amazon

16122092R00140